Gaelic In Your Gob

Four Dozen English Words That Came from the
Scottish Highlands

By Michael Newton

Illustrations by Natalia Lopes

Foreword by Àdhamh Ó Broin

GAELIC IN YOUR GOB

Published 2021 by Saorsa Media / Ingram.

Paperback ISBN   978-0-9713858-4-9

... Mhair i fòs
'S cha téid a' ghlòir air chall
Dh'aindeon gò
Is mì-rùn nan Gall ...

... It (Gaelic) still survives
And its glory will not be lost
Despite the guile
And the ill-will of the non-Gaels.

Alasdair mac Mhaighstir Alasdair, *c.*1751

Foreword

I was brought up a first-language English speaker, despite living on the coast of Argyllshire in Scotland's West Highlands and claiming a direct mixture of Irish and Scottish Gaelic descent. From the earliest age I was aware of being surrounded by Gaelic place names, although by that time - the very end of the 1970s - there was but a small handful of local people left who could still speak the language itself.

Moving to Glasgow with my mother to attend school, I was then exposed to the Scots language in the playground, especially during my years at secondary school and had to learn fast to survive! My father occasionally composed poetry in that tongue, and so it became a fixture in my life along with English. His experiences in the Second World War had caused him to remain in Germany where he had learned the local vernacular, later passing some of it to me. And so built up a pastiche of Germanic language that sparked an early interest in how each one related to the other.

After much encouragement from my MacLeod grandmother, I finally reclaimed the Gaelic language of my own people, reuniting ethnicity with language, and very soon started to note with great pleasure how much influence she had exacted on Lowland Scots vocabulary and grammar - most often entirely unbeknown to Lowlanders! What I hadn't realised - and as we are about to find out - is that a considerable amount of this vocabulary has seeped all the way through into modern English.

It must be ten years ago now that I first met Michael Newton. Before that, he was my favourite - albeit faceless - author on Scottish Gaelic matters. I was in Edinburgh on one of my many visits to the School of Scottish Studies when a mutual friend happened to inform me that they were just about to meet an old pal from across the water and that I would be welcome to join them. You can imagine my delight and excitement when it turned out who this friend was.

"Michael Newton," I remember musing upon finishing reading *A Handbook of the Scottish Gaelic World* a year or two before, "not the most Gaelic name I've ever heard." And yet this fellow's perspective had brought me closer to understanding the inner workings of my ancestral culture than I had yet managed to come.

Meeting Michael himself was no less a joy. I realised within seconds just why he had managed to write the way he did. Here was the proverbial scholar of ferocity, a man with an uncompromising take on the truths he uncovered no matter how uncomfortable and yet now he had a friendly face; it was his humour and kindness that soon impressed me, not to mention an almost shocking fluency in idiomatic Gaelic.

This book combines Michael's scholarship with that humour. It showcases a delightfully gung-ho attitude to rabbit-hole dives into finer detail whilst retaining total intelligibility and reading pleasure for the person discovering the Scottish Gaelic language for the very first time or simply looking for a good old wander onto a less-beaten etymological track.

Before teaching other languages to speakers of English, the late, great Michel Thomas would first identify the words in their target tongue that also appeared in their own - or at least had a recognisable equivalent - alerting new language learners to the foot they already had in the door. If your sights have been set on acquiring Scottish Gaelic, you couldn't make a better start than this little book, showing that for all its seeming exotic remoteness to the modern English speaker, a surprising number of our Gaelic words have in fact been in your gob all along.

Gun còrd an leabhar ruibh!

Àdhamh Ó Broin
Glasgow, Scotland
St Andrew's Day 2020

Introduction

Languages are like the air we breathe. As we absorb a language in our childhood, we unconsciously wrap sound and meaning together, soon coming to assume that it must be only natural that a tall, branching, leafy plant should be called "tree." Language and thought are so closely entwined in our minds that it can be hard for us to recognize the distinction between the two and remember that language has been created by human communities over many generations in ways that are essentially arbitrary rather than reflecting some principle of nature.

Languages are like biological species that evolve and spawn new generations of children over time. English has modern siblings in the Western Germanic branch of languages, including Dutch, Frisian, German, and Luxembourgish, and more distant relations in the Northern Germanic branch of languages, including Swedish, Norwegian, Danish, Icelandic, and Faroese. Like mutations in DNA that are passed along to descendants and signify distinctions from distant cousins, language branches are usually marked by systematic changes such as pronunciation, word meanings, grammar, and so on. Over time, these changes accumulate and work their way through other aspects of the language, sometimes causing unexpected side-effects. A single tree can spawn a forest in which every new generation carries elements of its parent but is subtly different, leading to an amazing range of diversity over the long term.

Languages are like museums that store relics of the history of the people who speak them and the interactions that they have had with other people who speak other tongues. Languages pick up new words as speakers coin new terms to describe ideas and objects that they discover themselves, and as they come into contact with unfamiliar ideas and objects belonging to other communities who already have names for them. The original source for those names may be quickly forgotten, however, even if the traces of exchanges between different language communities may remain in the words that linger in the mouths of speakers and in the texts they write - if they have a written form of their language.

This book offers insights into the relations between the Gaelic-speaking world of the Scottish Highlands and the English-speaking world by examining a selection of English words that have been borrowed from Scottish Gaelic, or at least influenced by it. Each of these words is explored in an essay that illuminates its meaning and usage in English and Scottish Gaelic, and an investigation into the means by which it entered the vocabulary of English speakers, or influenced a pre-existing word, so as to validate the claim that the English word owes something to its Gaelic relative.

It is natural for people to notice the similarity between words they know and those in other languages, and to speculate on the relationships between them. The exercise of determining those relationships is far more complicated than the untrained layperson might expect, however. For one, there is a fairly high probability that a word in one language will resemble some word in another language, regardless of their meanings and origins. After all, humans make a limited range of sounds, so there are bound to be words in other languages that remind us of ones that we know. Linguists call such unrelated pairs "false friends." Finding a word in English that resembles one in Gaelic may simply be a coincidence rather than an example of borrowing between them.

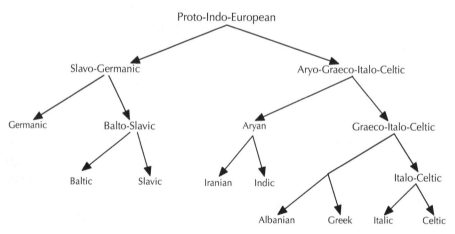

Figure 1: An early model of the Indo-European language family.

Another complication is that English and Gaelic are distant cousins: they are both members of the extended Indo-European language family of languages. Although English is a branch of the Germanic family, and Gaelic is a branch of the Celtic family, linguists theorize that they are descendants of an ancestral language that existed thousands of years ago, usually called "Proto-Indo-European" (see Figure 1). As a result, some of the words in English that resemble those in Gaelic are actually descended from a common root and hence still bear a family resemblance. Linguists call such word pairings "cognates." The cognate in Gaelic for the word "mother" in English, for example, is - wait for it - *màthair*. The apple has not fallen far from the tree, in this case.

Yet another trap is the fact that, like many other modern European languages, both Gaelic and English borrowed many words from Latin in the early medieval period (fifth to tenth centuries). Most of the terminology used in relation to the beliefs and practices of Christianity, including reading and writing, were borrowed from Latin. Although these loan words have continued to be subtly remolded over time, a general likeness usually remains. The English "clock" and the Gaelic *clog* "bell," for example, are both borrowings from Latin *clocca* "bell." The shift in meaning in English comes from the fact that bells were rung on the hour in the medieval monasteries, thus providing a form of time-keeping. Many more loanwords came into both Gaelic and English from Norman-French in the high medieval period (eleventh to fourteenth centuries).

These issues are explored by two formal branches of linguistics: philology, the study of the structures and historical development of languages and the relationships between them, and etymology, the study of the origin and evolution of words.

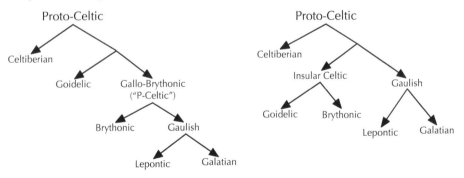

Figure 2: Two models of Celtic language family

The Celtic family of languages is a branch on the Indo-European tree. A medley of Celtic languages, descended from a theoretical ancestral language referred to as "Proto-Celtic," were spoken throughout central and western Europe at the beginning of the Christian era two thousand years ago. Evidence about these languages, like inscriptions on archaeological artifacts, and scholarship reconstructing them and the relationships between them, continue to accumulate, but our knowledge of the details of Celtic languages and peoples in ancient Europe is still inexact and the subject of vigorous debate.

There are, for example, two main models of the evolution of Celtic languages and the relationships between them, with arguments for and against each scenario they represent (see Figure 2). Irish, Manx, and Scottish Gaelic are the three child languages on the Goidelic branch of the Celtic language family. Welsh, Cornish, and Breton are the languages that survive on the Brythonic branch. Pictish was also a member of the Brythonic branch but during the early medieval period speakers of Pictish in Scotland began to speak the kindred Gaelic tongue, and left an imprint of Pictish influences on it. But let's rewind the clock again ...

At the dawn of recorded history, Britain and Ireland were occupied by Celtic-speaking communities. The Romans invaded Britain in 43 AD and dominated southern Britain until the early fifth century. Even though they did not attempt to invade or conquer Ireland, and failed to impose their rule on the north of Britain, Roman civilization brought lasting and significant cultural, social, economic, and political influences to the Gaels of Ireland and Scotland. Germanic peoples – Angles, Saxons, and Jutes – were entering the south and east of Britain both as soldiers hired by the Romans and as uninvited invaders by the fourth century AD. The Norse were attacking the communities along the shores of the Atlantic by the late eighth century and began settling their own competing colonies in the ninth. Britain has thus been home to a multitude of language communities competing for land and power for the last two thousand years. Words have ricocheted between them as much as weapons of war.

Gaels – members of Gaelic-speaking communities – have always been curious about the meanings and origins of new words that they encounter, and some have shown great creativity by attempting to explain words in other languages as though they consisted of Gaelic elements. Robert McDougall emigrated from Highland Perthshire to the Huron Tract in Canada in 1836. In 1841 he published the first guide in Scottish Gaelic for other Highlanders considering the possibility of emigrating to Canada and attempted to allay their fears of going into the unfamiliar, and potentially hostile, territory of First Nations by likening their society to that of the Scottish Highlanders. McDougall provided fanciful explanations of native words and names through Gaelic etymologies: he derived moccasin from *mo chasan* ("my feet"), papoose from *pathadh-bus* ("thirsty-mouth"), Tecumsheh from *deagh-chuimse* ("excellent-aim"), Ottawa from *àth-a-tuath* ("northern ford"), and more. While these derivations are patently inaccurate, they were meant to demonstrate affinity between ethnic groups through affinity in language.

The difficulty of tracing the tracks of words from community to community with reliable evidence and scholarly rigor has not damped the enthusiasm of would-be sleuths without formal training in modern methods for doing so. Over the last three hundred years, some people have become obsessed with crackpot theories about one language or another - usually assumed to be "ancient" or "primitive," such as Hebrew, Sanskrit, or Gaelic - being the "mother" of all others. Such extravagant claims require a great deal of creativity on the part of the writer, but few readers in the general public have the linguistic background to question the contortions to which the evidence is subjected.

Take, for example, Charles Mackay (1812-89), a Scottish Lowland poet who published *The Gaelic Etymology of the Languages of Western Europe* in 1877. Mackay aimed to raise the lowly status of Scottish Gaelic by claiming a stake for it in something which enjoyed high social prestige: the English language itself.

> First, that the Gaelic and other divisions of the Keltic, so despised by Johnson and the succeeding writers whom his false teaching led astray, prevails to a very large extent in the unliterary and colloquial speech of the English people, and that it continually crops up in apparently new, but in reality very ancient slang, or, as they are sometimes called, cant words.

> Second, that the Gaelic underlies all the languages of the Western, and some parts of North-Western Europe, especially French, Spanish, and Italian.

> Third, that what is called Anglo-Saxon, should be designated Kelto-Saxon, and that the word Angle, is a corruption of *An Gael*, or, "the Gael." ...

> In studying Gaelic we in reality go back to the earliest dawn of civilization. We find it to have been the language of a primitive, but a highly poetical,

and pure-minded people, who had attained a high degree of spiritual and moral culture.

As has often been the case, Mackay "proves" his thesis by neglecting more authoritative explanations of word origins and by bending the evidence to his will. His vexation at the mistreatment of Gaelic and its inexcusable neglect by English scholars opens the door to paranoid delusions and grandiose hyperbole unrestrained by diligent research methods. While he may have had justifiable reasons to rail against the stigmatization and dismissal of Gaelic, his mission to hijack English, rather than revitalize Gaelic and elevate it on its own terms, was a misguided use of his energy and creativity.

These exercises in delusion, laced with occasional truths, replay themselves from time to time. A similar mix of fact and farce can be seen in Daniel Cassidy's 2007 *How the Irish Invented Slang*, which attempts to explain American street vernacular by tracing a multitude of colloquialisms back to Irish. Cassidy did not enter the minefield of etymology through the orthodox gate of linguistic training but through the accident of being gifted a dictionary of modern Irish. As a result, he falls into the usual traps and pitfalls.

His strategy was to match up American-English words whose origin is listed as "unknown" with similar words or phrases in his dictionary, despite not being a speaker or scholar of the Irish language himself. He did, in a few cases, point to verified borrowings, but in most other cases Cassidy invents spurious connections that have been soundly rejected by experts. Some of those who see his enterprise as one elevating the Irish language take the criticism as an attack on their ethnic identity, which unfortunately does not help to promote clear thinking about the thorny issues of historical linguistics.

Cassidy's arguments were then, as they are now, mainly that the English and American lexicographers are biased against the Irish and don't want to give them their due, and that, in fact, the Irish were the source of much of our most common slang.

So, he decided he would fill the gap by finding obvious phonetic and orthographic similarities between Irish Gaelic and English-language slang. Which is, of course, a big heaping load of hooey. ...

Spelling and phonetic similarities must be looked at, but they are simply a starting point. They prove nothing. They merely provide a clue to be investigated by gathering evidence for and against the connection.

Evidence. Above all, Cassidy needs to support his claims with published evidence that shows the etymological path. Dated, continuous, in-context quotations from any written source will always be superior evidence over phonetic speculation based upon national, linguistic, or ethnic pride.

Any attempt to trace word histories has to consider the sound and sense of the word in both languages as well as demonstrate how the word was actually passed from one language community to the other. Alternative theories must be considered, which requires looking at a range of possible source languages. Etymology is an unforgiving endeavor and anyone entering it should do so with extreme caution. All of the borrowings I explore in this book have either been verified by previous scholars or at least suggested by them in the past. My main contribution is to flesh out these facts or suppositions with detailed background information from Gaelic sources.

Linguists have become increasingly aware of the messiness of the development of language and the inability of the conventional tree model to account fully for the many ways in which different languages interact and influence one another. One aspect of this complexity is that we cannot always assume that a word's origin and usage can be traced in a straight path to a singular source. When ordinary people encounter and use multiple languages, new words with multiple origins may be given birth or old, familiar words given new shades of meaning.

There are a number of words in English whose usage is likely to have been colored by a similar word in Gaelic, or whose primary origin may be Gaelic although it has grafted itself onto a similar word in English. False friends and cognates can merge and reinforce one another in the minds of speakers. Arthur Hutson argued in the 1940s that the loanword "shanty" is an amalgamation of at least two different words, Irish *sean-tigh* and French *chantier*.

> The word is too close in sound and meaning to *sean-tigh* to permit us to derive it from *chantier* alone. On the other hand, it is found in an area where the derivation from *chantier* is probable. I suggest that the word has two origins, the one Canadian French the other Irish. The meanings of *chantier* and *sean-tigh* are by a coincidence very close. Certainly neither the Irish nor the French abandoned their own word to borrow the other's. Possibly also shanty from *chantier* existed earlier than shanty from *sean-tigh*. But the latter on its arrival coalesced with the former reinforcing it,

extending its use to areas where it had not previously been known, and finally driving it out except perhaps in a limited area of its first occurrence.

The meanings, usages, and pronunciation of some Gaelic words overlap enough with words in English to argue for a place in their convoluted pedigrees, even if the Gaelic forms may not be their ancestors in an exclusive sense.

Wars of Words

Words are the very lifeblood of culture. Although external tokens - such as flags, clothing, and hair styles - may assert ethnic identities, it is language that gives societies internal cohesion by encoding their knowledge, sharing their ideas, expressing their histories, and transmitting the stories that articulate their unique place in the world. That is why empires typically attack the language of the people they wish to conquer and attempt to replace their language with the language of the empire.

The Gaelic peoples of Ireland and Scotland developed their own institutions of learning in the early medieval period and were very well served by them. The native élite of the Gaelic world adapted the tools of Latin learning to their own traditions and culture, maintaining beacons of scholarship that shone during the Dark Ages. Words were central to their many accomplishments. Gaels were the first people in Western Europe to develop their own vernacular literature, with prose and poetry, on both religious and secular topics, emerging between the late sixth and early eighth centuries. Educated Gaels took literacy and learning to the Anglo-Saxons in Britain and other peoples on the continent of Europe, and in some cases foreigners came to Gaelic centers of learning, such as Iona, for the specific purposes of receiving training in these skills.

From their earliest experimentation with literacy and literature, Gaels have shown an interest in dissecting words for their meaning and tracing their origins. Gaelic scholars have been creating glossaries that explain obscure and difficult words since the early medieval period. Although they used methods that do not meet modern standards - in fact, they succumbed to many of the same fallacies as modern amateurs, such as false friends - they demonstrated an awareness of linguistic evolution. Some of these ancient linguists even discovered some of the same etymological principles verified by modern scholars (such as the initial "f" of Gaelic words corresponding to the initial "v" of Latin cognates). Cormac Úa Cuilennáin, king-bishop of Cashel, is credited with producing *Sanas Cormaic* (often called *Cormac's Glossary* in English) in about the year 900, the earliest etymological dictionary of any vernacular European language.

Gaelic institutions of learning produced a range of books, tracts, and treatises on a variety of subjects - from linguistics to poetic meters, law, medicine, astronomy, and history - which had to be copied laboriously by hand on vellum manuscripts for centuries. Maintaining these systems of learning required the patronage of the native Gaelic aristocracy, whose political interests were intertwined with these institutions. They were deliberately targeted in both Scotland and Ireland for centuries by the expanding power of anglophone rivals, but the eradication of the Gaelic nobility in Ireland in the seventeenth century and the end of the clan system in Scotland during the eighteenth century brought the final collapse of the native orders of learned professionals.

This did not cause the complete loss of the literary and intellectual heritage of the past, however. First of all, the study of antiquities was emerging in anglophone circles and some of those scholars took an interest in the historical remains of the Celtic communities in the British Isles, even if these materials were not automatically afforded the same degree of prestige as anything labeled as Anglo-Saxon or Germanic.

One of the key figures in the development of modern Celtic Studies was Edward Lhuyd (1660-1709), a Welsh scholar who became curator at the Ashmolean Museum in Oxford. In about the year 1697 he visited every Celtic-speaking area of the British Isles and Brittany, meeting with surviving members of the learned orders, transcribing vocabulary and oral traditions in the Celtic languages, and collecting any ancient manuscripts he could find. One of the manuscripts Lhuyd acquired was a copy, made in Scotland by Eoghann MacGilleathain in 1698, of a glossary that explained obscure Gaelic words in poetry, originally composed in the fourteenth century by the Irish poet Seán Ó Dubhagáin. Even the task of expounding abstruse terminology was a subject fit for Gaelic poets!

In 1707 Lhuyd published the first volume of *Archaeologia Britannica: an Account of the Languages, Histories and Customs of Great Britain, from*

Travels through Wales, Cornwall, Bas-Bretagne, Ireland and Scotland but his death prevented any further volumes from appearing. Lhuyd laid the foundations for Celtic linguistics, observing the split between divergent branches of Celtic, and identifying forms of Celtic languages in Gaul and the Iberian peninsula as well as the British Isles.

Besides his own research, his volume also contains poems congratulating him for his efforts to restore the prestige of the Celtic languages by recovering their histories. Three of these are written in Scottish Gaelic by men who inherited manuscripts and elements of the medieval literary tradition. Robert Campbell of Cowall, for example, wrote:

... A ntabhair fa n'deirram shúd
Canamhuin or dhearc na nttír úd;
Air bhi dhi o shean a mbruid
A sgoileadh nois o chuibhreach ...
Neach da fheabhas 's fann a chor
'S canamhuin a bhi da easbhuidh ...

The reason why I say that
Is that the splendid language of those countries,
Having been for a long time in slavery
Has now been freed from its bondage ...
Anyone of whatever worth, his plight is feeble
If he lacks language ...

The ode by the Reverend John MacLean of Mull outlines the illustrious history of Gaelic, contrasting its misfortunes after the ascendency of anglophones in the royal Scottish court and positions of power. Lhuyd's mission, he asserts, was part of a divine plan to restore the Gaelic language to its proper place in Scottish life:

... B'i bhoide muinte' Luchd gach duthch' is teangth'
Chuir Gaill is Dubhghaill chuic' an tiulsa 'nclonn
Nois dhfolmhsi úainn gu tur, mo nuár 's mo chreach,
'S tearc luchd a gáoil, b' é sud an saó'al fa seach.
Thuit í sann túr, maraon le hughdribh pfein,
'Sna Flaith' 'mbudh dúth í, ghabh do cumhdach speis.
Reic iád san chúirt í, air cáint úir o Nde,
'S do thréig le hair budh nár leo ngcán'mhain fein.
Air sár o Líath, biodh ádh, is cuimhnu' is buáidh,
Do rinn gu húr a dusgadh as a huáimh ...

... It was the mentor of people of every land and language,
Norsemen and Saxons sent children over to Iona.
Now, alas! we have lost it completely:
Gaelic has few devotees. What a somersault the world has taken!
It has fallen from the Tower, together with its own authorities
And its royal heirs, who once gave it shelter.
They sold it in the court for yesterday's upstart,
And scornfully abandoned it: ashamed of their own language.
Good luck, fame and success to the great Lhuyd
Who has roused Gaelic afresh from its grave ...

These learned men not only knew about the history of the Gaelic people and language as scholars, they recognized the power of language and the relationship between language and political power.

Besides assisting others who were studying antiquities in the anglophone world, some native Gaels attempted to salvage what they could from the wreckage of their own ancestral past from the inside. One of the greatest champions of this cultural reclamation project was Alasdair mac Mhaighstir Alasdair, best known as the chief poet-propagandist of the 1745 Jacobite Rising and Gaelic tutor to Prince Charles Edward Stuart. Educated at the University of Glasgow not long after the Treaty of Union in 1707, he also had extensive knowledge of the older Classical Gaelic practices, transcribed texts from the dwindling lines of poets and storytellers, and made use of traditional literary materials in his own innovative compositions. In 1751 he became the first Gaelic poet to print a volume of his own poetry.

Alasdair titled his volume *Ais-eiridh na Sean chánoin Albannaich* (The Resurrection of the Ancient Scottish Language), arguing for the revitalization of the Gaelic language as part of a wider project of Scottish cultural reinvigoration. The poem that opens his book is in praise of Gaelic, one that reveals his awareness of the emerging field of historical linguistics and his hopes that scholarship could help to elevate the status of the maligned language of ancient Scotland. He also indulges in dramatic boasts, self-consciously and intentionally, like claiming that Gaelic does not need to borrow words from other languages and that it was spoken in the Garden of Eden. Regardless of these hyperboles, he praises the many virtues of the language, the heroes who spoke it in the past, and its resilience in the face of long hardship in Scotland:

... Mhair i fòs
'S cha téid a' ghlòir air chall
Dh'aindeon gò
Is mì-rùn nan Gall.
'S i labhair Alba
'S galla-bhodaiche féin,
Ar flaith, ar prionnsaidh'
'S ar diùcanna gun éis.
An taigh-comhairl' an rìgh,
Nuair shuidheadh air binn a' chùirt,
'S i 'Ghàidhlig lìomhtha
Dh'fhuasgladh snaoim gach cùis.
'S i labhair Calum
Allail a' Chinn Mhóir,
Gach mith is maith
Bha 'n Alba, beag is mór ...

... It still survives
And its glory will not be lost
Despite the guile
And the ill-will of the non-Gaels.
It is what Scotland spoke,
And even the Lowland rascals,
Our nobility, our princes,
And our dukes, flawlessly.
In the king's chamber
When the court would be set in session,
It is polished Gaelic
That would solve the crux of each issue.
It is what illustrious
Malcolm Canmore spoke,
Every commoner and noble-person
Who was in Scotland, great and small ...

As the eighteenth century progressed, the church clergy became increasingly involved in developing Gaelic literature of various sorts. This was, in part, due to the practical limitation that few people outside of the church were literate in Gaelic. It was also, however, an intentional strategy on the part of the church establishment to attend to the people of the Scottish Highlands, who they generally considered not just unorthodox but practically pagan and in desperate need of improvement and reformation in order to conform to the demands of contemporary anglophone society. This could only be accomplished by providing religious texts in the only language that most Highlanders could understand - Gaelic - and by creating schools where they could be trained to read and write, with the ultimate goal of weaning them off of their native tongue and assimilating them into the anglophone world.

The Book of Common Order had been translated into Classical Gaelic in 1567 under the patronage of the Earl of Argyll, and a couple of other religious texts followed in the next century or so. The systematic translation of standard church readings into vernacular Scottish Gaelic, however, including the Bible itself, did not begin until the 1750s. Even then, finding people with suitable training was a challenge, and the lack of a dictionary for the modern language was seen as a fundamental shortcoming. Alasdair mac Mhaighstir Alasdair produced a basic Gaelic-English vocabulary list for the schools run by the Society in Scotland for Propagating Christian Knowledge that was published in 1741, but it was very limited in scope. Dugald Buchanan petitioned for support in 1767 to compile a dictionary to accompany his translation of the New Testament, to explain words and concepts with which his Highland readers would not be familiar.

The first full Gaelic-to-English dictionary was published in 1780 by the Reverend William Shaw, although it included many terms in Irish and hence did not reflect vernacular Scottish Gaelic usage entirely accurately. Other church ministers made further attempts to publish authoritative dictionaries of the language in 1795, 1815, 1825, 1831, 1842, and 1845.

The most important and comprehensive Gaelic-to-English dictionary compiled in the past, however, was published in sections between 1902 and 1911 by Edward Dwelly (1864-1939), an Englishman who acquired a zeal for Gaelic while serving as a bagpiper in the British Army and fieldworker with the Ordinance Survey. His dictionary, which has over 77,000 headwords, was a massive undertaking for a single person and is still the most widely-used printed dictionary among modern readers and writers of Scottish Gaelic.

The Celtic languages in general - Irish and Scottish Gaelic included - have suffered greatly for many generations from undue prejudice and neglect in the modern academy, as elsewhere in anglophone society. Governments and educational institutions have invested heavily for over two centuries in training scholars about the minutiae of the English language, and in collecting and scrutinizing the materials necessary to conduct scholarship about its historical development, while simultaneously failing to provide similar support for their Celtic-speaking constituencies until very recently.

A team of professional scholars began work in 1857 on what became the *Oxford English Dictionary*, a comprehensive historical dictionary of English that traces the meanings and histories of every word in the language. Portions of the volume began to be printed in 1884 but it was not until 1928 that the first round of the effort was completed. Then, as now, the scholars involved had much better training in Germanic and Romance languages than Celtic ones. This is not surprising, as the study of Celtic languages has been slow and unsteady in its development due to the marginalized status of the language communities and the constant drain of resources by and into English. The chair of Celtic at Oxford University was not established until 1876 and the chair of Celtic Studies in Scotland, with a special focus for Scottish Gaelic, until 1882. As a result, the influences of various forms of Gaelic on English dialects have certainly not received the attention they deserve. As long ago as 1888, William Mackay complained:

> But why should not English philologists take the trouble, as the German philologists do, of learning the Celtic languages thoroughly? It is much more their interest than that of the Germans and it is a far more patriotic course, for the Celts form a part of the United Kingdom.

Fortunately, recent initiatives leveraging state-of-the-art technologies have moved the study of the history of Gaelic forward quickly and onto the internet. I have relied heavily upon these tools to carry out the research necessary to illustrate the evidence of Gaelic-to-English word histories and cannot imagine attempting this book without them.

DASG, a bilingual acronym which stands for *Digital Archive of Scottish Gaelic* in English and *Dachaigh Airson Stòras na Gàidhlig* in Gaelic, has been a key resource in my efforts. DASG was initiated at the University of Glasgow in 2006 and has already assembled a digital corpus of over 20 million words from primary sources, supplemented with fieldwork done between the 1960s and 1980s, for the long-term goal of creating an historical dictionary of Scottish Gaelic. *The Dictionary of the Scots Language* is a parallel project launched in 2002 that also builds upon previous research materials and offers an online interface to access a wealth of texts and word histories about Lowland Scots. It has been another constant companion on my lexical quests.

Am Faclair Beag ("The Little Dictionary") has also been a pillar of my research. *Am Faclair Beag* is an online Gaelic-English-Gaelic dictionary that emerged as a grass-roots collaboration between Michael Bauer and Will Robertson. The initial goal in 1999 was to digitize the comprehensive dictionary produced by Edward Dwelly. No sooner was that accomplished than they began to accumulate further words and idioms from other sources. Their extensive and versatile resource now has over 110,000 entries and serves an average of 5,000 to 6,000 word searches a day.

Another of the essential tools upon which I have relied is *eDIL* (*Electronic Dictionary of the Irish Language*), incorporating Gaelic texts from the period c.700-c.1700, inclusive of Scottish Gaelic materials. During this era, after all, Gaelic speakers were living across the archipelago of islands from the north of Scotland to the south of Ireland, engaging in a common language and literary tradition that resounded in the halls of chieftains as much as in the cottages of the peasantry.

The internet has created the ability to coordinate massively collaborative efforts to gather raw data and linguistic methods. I've also benefited from the etymological notes available on *Wiktionary*, an open-source dictionary containing valuable linguistic materials.

Language Contact and Exchange

The proposition of this book - that words can be found in English that originate in Scottish Gaelic - is actually a more gnarly issue that it may initially appear. It raises questions such as, What do we mean by "English"? Which English? English is not a single monolithic language, but since its beginnings in Roman Britain has been spoken across widely scattered communities in a variety of dialects. English-speaking colonists first settled in Ireland in the twelfth century and in North America in the seventeenth century.

Various forms of English have continued to evolve in these communities, separately, in distinctive local forms, but also in constant contact. Is English a single language or a series of dialects? Should the Germanic language spoken in the Scottish Lowlands, commonly referred to as "Scots," be considered a dialect of English or an entirely separate language? The answers to these questions have as much to do with social status, political sovereignty, and personal agendas as they do objective linguistic criteria.

A similar set of questions revolves around Scottish Gaelic: when did Gaelic acquire distinctively Scottish features that distinguished it from the forms of Gaelic spoken in Ireland? Even the use of the name "Gaelic" can be controversial in Ireland because it implies a divorce between language and national identity, even though this is actually the name of the language in Gaelic itself and makes it easier to associate it with its sister language in Scotland. Despite this shared heritage and a great deal of shared vocabulary, I have tried to avoid claiming words that are known to have been borrowed via Irish rather than Scottish Gaelic, even if they are as familiar to Scottish Gaels as to Irish Gaels. Such words include slew (from *sluagh* "a crowd"), shamrock (from *seamróg*), brogue (from *bróg* "shoe"), and puss (from *bus* "front of the mouth").

It is sometimes difficult to distinguish between the contributions of Irish and Scottish Gaelic. Take the word "curse" in English. The most recent appraisal is that it was the result of borrowing Gaelic *cúrsagaid* "correct, chastise, rebuke" into Old English with the added cross-fertilization of the Latin *cursus* "a set of prayers or ritual formula." The evidence suggests that the Gaelic term was used in the church centers of Northumbria and then spread southward into other dialects of Old English. The conversion of Northumbria to Christianity was largely due to the work of the monks of Iona who established themselves in Lindisfarne in about 634 AD and remained dominant there for generations, even extending their influence further afield in England.

The monastery at Iona had been founded by Saint Columba in about the year 563 in territory that is now considered Scottish. Gaelic was the dominant native language of the majority of those who lived there. We do not have clear evidence that there were significant divergences yet between the forms of Gaelic spoken in Ireland and Scotland in this era, so it would seem to stretch the facts to try to claim "curse" as one of the borrowings from Scottish Gaelic to English even if Iona would seem safely within Scotland's borders by today's reckoning.

Despite this reservation, I have chosen to include the very early borrowing of Gaelic *Scot* into Latin to give us the modern term for the

Scots, given that this is such an important and fundamental word in our vocabulary about Scotland as a whole.

Some of the words borrowed from Scottish Gaelic were themselves earlier loans from other languages, such as Brythonic (the parent language of Welsh) and Latin, so the chain of transference demonstrates the permeable and unstable nature of language, language communities, and the boundaries we draw between them.

The tiny remnant of Gaelic speakers left in Scotland today, and their diminished social and political weight, gives many people the false impression that the language is of no great historical consequence, but it is a mistake to ignore the longstanding presence of Gaels in Scotland. About a third of Scots spoke Gaelic at the beginning of the eighteenth century, and native Gaelic families survived on fringes of the Lowlands in areas such as Dunbartonshire and Aberdeenshire into the twentieth century. Linguistic and literary evidence about these Gaelic communities is still slowly emerging from archives and attics.

It should not be surprising that Scottish Gaelic has had its greatest impact on the anglophones who have lived closest to the Scottish Highlands, namely, the people of the Scottish Lowlands. Despite whatever distrust and hostility have existed across the Highland-Lowland divide during the course of centuries, Gaels and Anglophones have traded goods, married one another, signed contracts, shared interests, formed bonds, and held conversations that resulted in mutual linguistic influences.

There are many ways in which Scottish Gaelic words have entered into the vocabulary of English speakers at different places and times but the case of the Lowland Scots language is unique. The Lowlands were largely Gaelic-speaking in the twelfth century, when the region was colonized by speakers of Germanic languages in burghs and other centers of Anglo-Norman power (see Figure 3 and the entries SCOT and SASSENACH). Gaelic slowly gave way to Lowland Scots between the twelfth and fourteenth centuries in these areas. Some influence is simply the result of the native Gaelic speakers retaining older words and speech patterns as they became Scots speakers.

As the Gaelic scholar Lachann MacBheathain remarked in the early twentieth century, the relationship between Highlands and Lowlands of Scotland has been complex, and has conditioned the ways in which the corresponding languages and cultures of the regions have interacted with one another:

Nuair a thachair a' Ghàidhlig agus Beurla nan Gall air fonn na h-Albann, cha b'ann le fàilte no le furan. Cha d'thàinig am bàigh an cois an dàimh, oir bha eadar-dhealachadh 'n an àladh agus 'n an eachdraidh. Ach, thuit orra a bhi anns an aon tìr mar choimhearsnaich, agus tha a buaidh féin aig a' choimhearsnachd. Is fheudar do'n chomh-ursainneach a bhi 'n a chomh-mharsannach, agus a bhi a' malairt eismeil agus choingheall.

Eadar an dà chànain so, ma ta, tha a' choimhearsnachd fada, agus ged nach 'eil a' mharsannachd anabarrach tha a luach féin aice. Ghabh a' Ghàidhlig iomadh nì o'n Ghalldachd, agus gu tric gun fhàth sam bith ach neònachas, agus cha do dhiùlt a' Bheurla gu buileach dol an eismeil na Gàidhealtachd.

When Gaelic and Lowland Scots encountered one another on Scottish soil, it was not with a warm welcome and embrace. Affection did not accompany this relationship, as there was a difference in their development and history. But they were neighbors in the same land, and the community bears the influence of that very influence. Someone who lives under the same roof must be a fellow broker, exchanging mutual dependencies and debts.

The community has a long history with both of these two languages, then, and although there is not a large amount of exchange, it has its own value. Scottish Gaelic took many things from the Lowlands, often with no reason but uniqueness, and English did not entirely refuse becoming indebted to the Highlands.

Given that the Lowland Scots has also been slow to get the financial and institutional support it needs to develop a formal and detailed analysis of its history, revelations about the influence of Scottish Gaelic have been slow and uneven in coming to light. Lowland Scots has been fertilized over the centuries by scores of words that have originally come from Gaelic or been shaded by it, as evidenced by such terms as garron, messan, capercaillie, finnock, gaberlunzie, caird, clabber, and sonsie. For the purposes of discussion in this book I have chosen loans into Scots that are known widely outside of Scotland itself, but there are many others in the daily speech of specific regions of the Lowlands.

People writing accounts in English about Highland communities in their native territory, and the artifacts and practices unique to them, needed appropriate words and sometimes simply adapted them directly from Gaelic in their accounts. This is especially true for landscape terms such as BOG, CRAG, LOCH, corrie, machair, strath, glen, kyle, and so on.

This also happened with social structures and cultural customs that anglophones encountered, such as CLAN, SLOGAN, CATERAN, and BELTANE. Gaelic legal terms that were borrowed into Scots demonstrate that aspects of a Celtic law system - customary and formal - that parallel those in Ireland were inherited widely in Scotland, illustrated by such words as tocher (from *tochradh* "dowry"), slains (from *slán* "indemnity"), colpindach (from *colpthach* "fee paid in cattle"), cain (from *cáin* "tribute"), and conveth (from *coinnmed* "billeting").

It is not unusual for fragments of heritage languages to remain in communities that switch to speaking English predominantly, especially in the form of slang, idiomatic expressions, and terms of affection within families. Whether as immigrants to cities in the Lowlands or in overseas colonies, few Highlanders maintained their mother tongue past the first generation, but echoes of the old tongue sometimes lingered.

In general, Scottish Gaelic-speaking immigrants seem to have contributed surprisingly little to the dialects of English used in their new home regions. There is virtually no trace of Gaelic in the English of descendants of the settlers who once formed the largest community of Scottish Highlanders in the United States, the Cape Fear region of the Carolinas. Despite that, there is intriguing evidence of at least some Scottish Gaelic influence in American English.

The legacy of the Scottish Gaelic language in North America, moreover, is not restricted to just a few pockets of white folk in rural settlements. There are numerous examples of people of African descent who were fluent Gaelic speakers as well as virtuosos of Highland musical tradition. This was largely, although not exclusively, the result of the enslavement of Africans by Gaelic speakers. A Scottish minister who served a congregation of freed slaves after the Civil War in North Carolina remarked in 1872, for example: "I have met with a number of coloured people who speak the Gaelic as well as if they had been raised in any of the Hebrides."

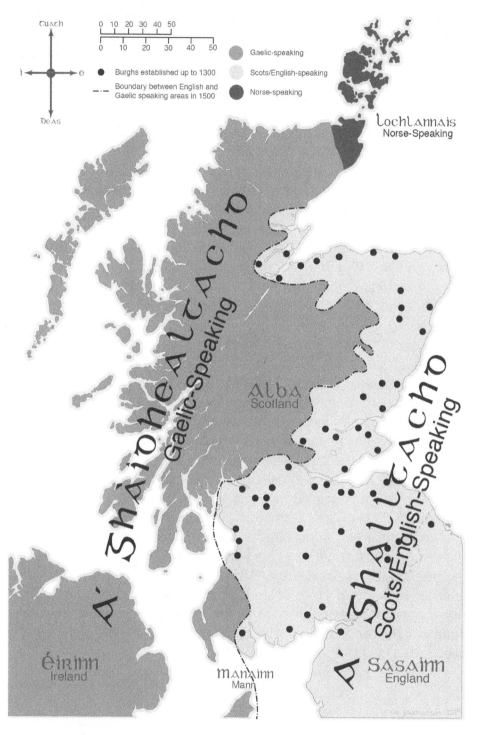

Figure 3: Map of language areas in 16th-century Scotland

The circle widens even further when considering the intermarriage of Gaelic-speaking fur traders with the native peoples of North America. A Scottish minister visiting the North-West Territory of Canada in the late nineteenth century observed (in terms that are offensive by today's standards) not only that Gaelic survived among the children of fur traders but that they valued the connection that the language gave them to the Highlands and that it formed an important part of their identity:

> He states that many of the half-breeds talk splendid Gaelic, and if asked where they came from they name some place in Lewis, though they have never seen Scotland. The explanation of this is that their fathers, who were Hudson Bay Company's servants, and had married squaws, hailed from Lewis. The half-breed is proud of his Gaelic, as he thinks it connects him with his father's country, of which he is also proud.

Just a handful of words of Gaelic origin seem to remain in the English spoken in communities of the Eastern Maritimes of Canada, where there are still native Gaelic speakers some five or more generations after the arrival of the original immigrants. Although referring to a musical instrument belonging to Aboriginal Australians, the term "didgeridoo" itself may have been coined by Gaelic-speaking settlers in Australia in the form *dùdaire dubh* or *dùdaiche dubh* "black horn." But these are the noteworthy exceptions that defy the general pattern.

The influence of written literature in English, especially poetry and fiction, in disseminating words of Gaelic origin cannot be overstated. The novels and poems of Walter Scott in particular were highly popular around the world and were instrumental in popularizing words to a much larger audience than possible through direct, inter-personal contact between Gaelic speakers and anglophones. It's also important to recognize that popular literature, especially books and poems by Walter Scott, sometimes presented Highland life in a sympathetic light and may have made English speakers more receptive to these words and less likely to reject them as beneath their notice.

The Gaelic loan words selected for this volume have been arranged into seven different categories: People and Names; Community and Customs; Warfare; Sport and Music; Food and Domestic Life; Landscape and Nature; Slang and Idioms. I have ordered the words within each section so as to expand upon the nature of the history and meaning of words, rather than according to alphabetical order or strict chronology. This seems to me to be the most fruitful way of grouping this material, but other ways of organizing it are possible, such as the means by which borrowings happened, the time period, part of speech, and so on.

The vignettes in this volume demonstrate the obvious truth that various forms of Gaelic and English have been jostling one another for centuries, both within the British Isles and in overseas colonies. These languages, and speakers of them, did not meet on a level playing field but one on which English was the language of power, prestige, and privilege, intended to provide every advantage and reward. This goes a long way toward explaining why the impact of Celtic languages on English in general has been largely muted.

Although these word histories open windows into these convoluted intersections between Scottish Gaeldom and the anglophone world, they are not intended to argue for any special or exclusive place for Gaelic in the story of English. That would be a fool's errand. Scottish Gaelic has its own story and its own wealth of linguistic riches. It is a tree worthy of honoring in the old growth forest of human culture, one that gave sustenance and shelter to throngs of poets and singers before its limbs were hacked and its roots poisoned. It still survives, despite centuries of ill-treatment, and perhaps if finally given the care and respect it deserves, it will issue new shoots of growth and bring forth new words yet unspoken. To quote again from an early twentieth-century Gaelic scholar:

> Tha an diugh mór abhainn na cànain Shasunnaich mar dhìle leathainn air a h-at le uisge o iomadh eileach, agus air a h-uallachadh agus a tacadh le cònlach tiugh de nithibh gun àireamh a tha a' snàmh air a h-aghaidh - ionnsachadh is innealan iongantach nan làithean a tha ann. Cha dean sinn tàir air an tuil ud, no idir air allt eòlach na Beurla Ghallda a tha a' glugan agus a' crònan mu dhorus cèardaich a' bhaile bhig. Ach, tha fìor-uisge na Gàidhlig mar shruth fallan nam beann, a' sìor-mhonmhur mu na nithibh àrda o'n d'thàinig e, agus làraichean ar n-aithrichean. Ma tha sinn duineil agus dualach, òlaidh sinn a ghnàth ùr neart agus slàinte á lànachd an t-sruith so. Ma bhitheas sinn dleasnach agus dligheil 'n ar ginealach, le tùr tionnsgalach, bheir sinn fa near gu'n cumar an sruth so làn agus glan, gu bhi a ghnàth mar amar-àiteachaidh a' comh-roinn beartais a bheatha am fad agus am fagus, ionnus gu'm buanaich, cha'n e a mhàin Albainn, ach iomadh sluagh agus teanga o bhuaidh àghaich na Gàidhlig, oir is deimhin gu'm faigh iad feartan uaithe-se nach fhaigh iad gu bràth á fuaran eile.

Nowadays the great river of English is like a wide deluge that has been swollen with waters from many dams and that has been burdened and choked by a dense flotsam of innumerable items that float on its surface - the marvelous learning and innovations of modernity. We will not disparage that flood, nor the familiar stream of Lowland Scots that gurgles and croons about the smithy-door of the hamlet. But, the pure waters of Gaelic are like the wholesome stream of the mountains, constantly murmuring about the high things from which it came, and the traces of our forefathers. If we are dutiful and adhere to tradition, we will always drink fresh strength and health from the fullness of this stream. If our generation is responsible and dutiful, with innovative ingenuity, we will make it our intention to keep this stream full and clean, so that it will always be as a pool of cultivation that shares the wealth of life near and far, so that not only Scotland may flourish, but many peoples and languages, from the prosperous influence of Gaelic, for verily they will find virtues in it that they will never obtain from any other wellspring.

I am deeply grateful for the assistance of people who gave me useful information and advice about the many details involved in writing these word histories, especially Michael Bauer, Andrew Breeze, Ian Clayton, Phil Jamison, Jake King, Shannon MacMullin, Christopher Scott Thompson, Patrick Wadden, and Alex Woolf. Àdhamh Ó Broin offered many interesting reflections on word usages between Gaelic, Scots and English to me, and I am also thankful to him for writing the foreword. The map of language divisions in Scotland was illustrated by Críostóir Piondargás.

Most of the words in this collection have been assiduously investigated by etymologists in the past, but there are several that I include whose likely Gaelic derivation was suggested by Raghnall MacGilleDhuibh of Peebles, Scotland, who was one of my instructors when I studied at the University of Edinburgh. These words are BOOGIE, BORE, BRASH, CROON, DIG / TWIG, GROTTY, and JILT. MacGilleDhuibh deserves special recognition and gratitude for his life-long dedication to Gaelic research which has both revealed many of the riches of tradition and enriched these roots for the generations to come.

Michael Newton
Chapel Hill, North Carolina

People and Names

Scot

Are you proud to be Scottish? What does Scottishness mean? Who were the original Scots? We may perceive ethnicity as being stable and easy to recognize, especially because the modern myths of race reassure us that ethnic identity is inscribed in DNA. Human beings like to be able to divide the world into clear and firm categories but as a matter of fact, ethnic groups, the perceptions of them, and the names for them change over time. The features or conditions that make particular social groups distinctive or enable them to maintain their cohesion come and go: communities may lose their land, migrate, and mingle with a different ethnic group, or they may be conquered and absorbed by an incoming group in their own land, or they may adopt new ways of thinking about themselves and their relationships to their neighbors. All of these usually cause a change in the names that people use for themselves or that others use for them. The words used to identify the land of Scotland and the people who have lived there reflect major shifts through the centuries such as these.

The word *Scotti* (also spelled *Scoti*) first appears in Latin sources of the fourth century AD in close association with the island of Ireland and its people, but in a way that suggests some distinction. A Latin document written c. AD 312 known as *Nomina Provinciarum Omnium* lists Roman provinces and the non-Roman enemies of these occupied territories, and includes the *Scoti* along with the *Picti* and *Caledonii*. These latter two tribes were Celtic peoples living in Britain north of the Roman-occupied zone. Ammianus Marcellinus, who died some time between 390 and 400, wrote a Latin history stating that the *Scotti* and *Picti* attacked the frontiers of Roman Britain in the 360s.

St Patrick's Epistle, probably written in the late fourth or early fifth century, uses the term *Scotti* distinct from the term for the land and people of Ireland, suggesting that not all people with a Gaelic ethnic identity lived in Ireland. And Patrick mentioned *Scotti* and *Picti* together in a British geographical context in a way similar to earlier Roman writers.

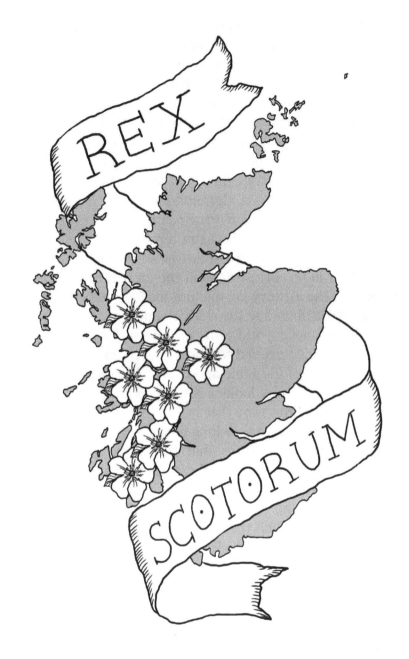

Although we do not know the origin of the kin-group name *Scotti* for certain, it does not appear to have been created by the Romans from Latin. Some scholars have argued that it likely came from the Gaelic word *scot(h)* "flower, blossom; (finest) choice, premier." The upper classes of Gaelic society are likely to have used it to describe themselves, and they would have used the booty from raids on Roman Britain to elevate their social and economic status within their own communities. The Romans seem to have borrowed this self-promotional designation directly from Gaelic and later writers continued using this term in Latin.

The element *scot-* appears in some Old Celtic personal names and the later form of the word, rendered as *scoth* or *scath*, appears in medieval Gaelic texts with appropriate connotations. In a poem describing an opulent Christmas feast held in 1351, to which artists from all over the Gaelic world were invited, Gofraidh Fionn Ó Dálaigh praises the host, Uilleam Ó Ceallaigh, as *scath Breagh* ("the scion of Brega").

Literate Gaels took up the Latin term *Scotti* to refer to themselves, especially when writing in Latin. One of the only surviving historical texts written in the British Isles in the early medieval period, *Historia Brittonum* "The History of the Britons," written in Latin *c.*830 and traditionally attributed to the cleric Nennius, indicates that the bookish monks of the Gaelic world were already working on a myth to explain their origins. They needed to find a way to insert themselves into the accepted stories of the Bible and Classical world, and, like most other peoples, they did it by looking for names that resembled their own – thus showing, by the way, that bad etymology has been practiced by respectable people for a very long time!

Historia Brittonum claims that the Scots are descended from a Scythian nobleman based on the similarity between the two names *Scythi* and *Scotti*. Gaelic scholars continued to elaborate these origin legends and by the mid-ninth century had invented a high-status character named Scota, the daughter of Pharaoh, king of Egypt, from whom the Scoti were said to descend.

The territory that we now know as "Scotland" was occupied by a patchwork of different communities in the early medieval period. The kingdom of Dál Riata was established no later than the sixth century, bridging the north of Ireland to Argyll. The Gaelic language and culture received a signal boost through the early political strength of Dál Riata. Pictish and Dál Riatic dynasties became entangled with one another and by the eighth century some Pictish kings had Gaelic names and held Pictish and Dál Riatic kingships at the same time.

The spread of Gaelic into the north of Britain was accelerated by the church founded by Saint Columba of Iona, whose clergy who were predominantly Gaelic-speaking. The arts - literature, architecture, the visual arts, and so on - reached high levels of accomplishment under the patronage of the church with a distinctly Gaelic flavor and enabled acculturating the kings of Pictland even when they enjoyed political supremacy over rival Gaelic dynasties. The invasions of Vikings into the Dál Riatic territories of the west also expedited the movement of Gaels and their cultural influences eastward into areas of Pictish dominance.

Anglo-Saxon writers record the ethnic term *Scot* for kings of the Pictish kingdom in the tenth century, and the sons of King Malcolm III who became kings of Scotland used the Latin title *Rex Scotorum* "The King of the Gaels" for themselves, even while acknowledging that some of the communities of the realm were not ethnically Gaelic but English, French, and Galwegian. The term "Scot" continued to be understood to refer to the Gaelic language and its associated culture and identity into the thirteenth century. After the settlement and domination of the Anglo-Normans in Scotland in the twelfth century, however, it slowly became detached from an ethnically-specific meaning and gained more abstract geographical associations.

During the thirteenth and fourteenth centuries the Scottish Lowlands shifted from being largely Gaelic in speech and culture to absorbing a Germanic language closely related to English. The people of the Lowlands accordingly changed the terms they used for themselves and the Gaelic speakers of the kingdom, who were by that time largely confined to the Highlands and Western Isles. By the 1380s, the people of the Lowlands began to use the term "Irish" or "Erse" to refer to the Gaels and by the end of the fifteenth century they reframed the word "Scot" to refer to themselves rather than the Gaels.

The people who would have turned their heads to the exclamation "Great Scot!" changed greatly through the ages. From the fourth through the thirteenth centuries, *Scot(t)* referred specifically to Gaelic speakers, who left place names across the territory of Scotland from Galloway to Caithness. The Gaels are the original "Flowers of Scotland."

Sassenach

"Sassenach" is no doubt the word of Gaelic origin enjoying the greatest vogue in popular anglophone culture at the moment, having been brought into the spotlight of public attention through the success of Diana Gabaldon's *Outlander* series. One of the main characters, Claire Randall, is an English woman who finds herself magically transported to the eighteenth-century Highlands where Gaelic was the dominant language. James Fraser, the Gaelic-speaking Highlander who becomes her lover, calls her "Sassenach," which becomes a term of affection between them as their relationship blossoms.

The term "Sassenach" has thus become a kind of catchword for the highly popular *Outlander* franchise: not only do many fans sport items emblazoned with the word, but the actor who plays heart-throb Jamie Fraser has launched a brand of blended Scotch whisky named "The Sassenach."

It is widely recognized that the word "Sassenach" is a Gaelic borrowing into Scots that has derogatory connotations and that it is ultimately derived from the word "Saxon," the name of one of the three Germanic tribes who migrated to Britain along with the Angles and Jutes. Many modern scholars of Lowland Scots misunderstand and misrepresent the historical usage of the original term *Sasannach* in Gaelic, however. This may in part be due to being led astray by this statement in the 1771 novel *The Expedition of Humphrey Clinker* by Tobias Smollet: "The Highlanders have no other name for the people of the Low country, but Sassenagh, or Saxons." Despite being a native of Bonhill in West Dunbartonshire, which was on the Highland-Lowland divide in the eighteenth century, his explanation is quite off the mark.

As renowned Gaelic scholar John MacInnes explained in his 1989 article "The Gaelic Perception of the Lowlands," there is no evidence of *Sasannach* in Gaelic being applied to the people of the Lowlands, at least in normal and literal usage:

> The Gaelic for Scotland is *Alba*, and a Scot, no matter which part of Scotland he comes from, is an *Albannach*. The Gaelic for England is *Sasann* or *Sasainn* (slight dialectal variants); an Englishman is a *Sasannach*; 'Scotswoman' is *Ban-Albannach*; 'Englishwoman', *Ban-Sasannach*. ... No Scot, man or woman, can be 'Sasannach' or 'Ban-Sasannach', and that

applies with equal force to Highlanders and Lowlanders alike. A Lowlander (male) is a *Gall*; a Lowlander (female) a *Ban-Ghall*. ... The sharpness of the distinction that Gaelic tradition draws between Lowlander and Englishman is not always appreciated to the full by non-Gaels.

There are many examples of the use of the ethnic terms *Sasannach* and *Gall* in texts to demonstrate that this is indeed the most accurate way to understand how these terms have been used by Gaels for many centuries. Patrick Graham, the minister for Aberfoyle in Highland Perthshire, for example, recorded a story in the early nineteenth century explaining a place name near the Pass of Aberfoyle:

> In the time of the commonwealth, a party of Cromwell's army, attempting to penetrate into the upper country by this pass, was repulsed with considerable loss, by the natives, headed by the Earl of Glencairn, and Graham of Duchray, whose castle, situated about a mile to the southward, the invaders had just reduced to ashes.

> A little to the westward of the inn, one of Duchray's followers shot one of the Englishmen from the opposite side of the river, who fell near a clump of trees, by the road side, which is called to this day *Bad an t-Sasannaich*, or the Englishman's Clump; the term *Sasannach*, or Saxon, being uniformly applied by Highlanders, not to the inhabitants of the Low Country, but to Englishmen.

There are at least thirty-seven place names across the Highlands which contain the element *Sasannach*, and stories which explain these place names, that corroborate this usage. The term *Gall*, however, changed over time and this can cause confusion. Gaels used it in reference to the Norse between the ninth and twelfth centuries, during which time many areas around the Atlantic seaboards of Scotland and Ireland were colonized by settlers from Scandinavia. New names evolved later on in Gaelic, coupled with color terms *fionn* "fair" and *dubh* "dark," to distinguish the communities of Norse immigrants from the more recent colonists of the Lowlands who were referred to in Gaelic with the generic and unmarked term *Gall*. The exact chronology of, and reasons for, these linguistic developments are still unclear, even if the resulting usages in Gaelic by the late medieval period are.

Although "Sassenach" appeared in several anglophone texts written in Scotland during the eighteenth century, it was Walter Scott's highly popular novel *Waverly*, published in 1814, that introduced the word to a large reading audience. When it was picked up later in the nineteenth century by other anglophone writers, however, it was sometimes misinterpreted in the same way as Smollet did above, assuming that Highlanders made no distinction between Lowland Scots and English people. In his *History of Scotland*, published in 1867, for example, James MacKenzie stated: "A body of ten thousand Highlanders was mustered, half-savage clansmen from the mountains, hating with an ancient grudge the 'Sassenach', or Lowlanders."

Perhaps this expansion of the term reflects the affiliation felt by many in the Lowlands with fellow anglophones in England at a time when racial definitions of identity were dominant and Lowlanders were eager to tout their credentials as bona fide Anglo-Saxons rather than Celts. It does not, however, reflect the orthodox definition of the term in Gaelic.

At the same time, it is also important to recognize that Gaels sometimes used the term *Sasannach* in a disparaging tone to chastise the ethnic allegiances and pretensions of Lowlanders who were essentially indistinguishable from Englishmen. As John MacInnes again notes:

> Of course, there will be occasions when a Lowland Scot is mistaken for an Englishman. In this connection, it is noteworthy that until recent times at least sportsmen who came to the Highlands to stalk deer, shoot grouse and fish for salmon were generally referred to not as *Goill* (plural of *Gall*) but as *Sasannaich*. If they were in fact Lowlanders, the implication seems to be, they were Lowlanders in English disguise. This perception concerns social class and speech habits.

There is a number of examples of *Sasannach* being used in this sense in nineteenth-century Gaelic texts, especially in the context of Clearances and conflicts over identity, land, and authority in the Highlands. One of the most vehement statements of this sort comes from the poet *Màiri Mhór nan Òran* "Great Mary of the Songs," one of the most outspoken Gaelic voices of the later nineteenth century. In a song about her home in the Isle of Skye, she hopes that the *Sasannaich* will be cleared from the island in the same manner as her own people had been dispossessed:

Cuimhnichibh ur cruadal
Is cumaibh suas ur sròl,
Gun téid an roth mu'n cuairt duibh
Le neart is cruas nan dòrn;

Gum bi ur crodh air bhuailtean
'S gach tuathanach air dòigh,
'S na Sasannaich air fuadach
Á Eilean uain' a' Cheò.

Remember your hardship
And keep your banner aloft
Until the Wheel of Fortune turns in your favor
With the strength and hardness of fists;
Until your cattle are in the folds
And every crofter is well situated
And the *Sasannaich* have been expelled
From the green Isle of Mist.

Màiri and her audience knew that not all of those who had cheated the Gaelic peasantry, and usurped their land, were ethnically English, but the term *Sasannach* served as an oppositional identity.

There is a similar tone of disapproval in a prose dialog published in 1899 between two men discussing the future of the Gaelic language. One of the participants, Calum from Skye, is given the nickname *Sasannach* because he has no commitment to his Gaelic heritage. His rival in the debate says of him:

Tha e soilleir nach e Gàidheal ceart a th' annad. Tha thu na do nàmhaid do'n Ghàidhlig; agus air an adhbhar sin, chan eil e glic do Ghàidheal sam bith éisteachd riut, no do chomhairle a ghabhail. Tha do leithid-sa nas cunnartaiche do bheatha na Gàidhlig na nì sam bith eile a tha 'g obrachadh na h-aghaidh.

It is clear that you are not a proper Gael. You are an enemy of Gaelic; and for that reason, it is not wise for any Gael to listen to you, or to take your counsel. Your sort of person is more dangerous to the life of Gaelic than anything else that is working against it.

A Gaelic book published in 1845 about the 1745 Jacobite Rising also illustrates the rhetorical use of *Sasannach* in symbolic opposition to a Gaelic cultural allegiance. The author and his audience certainly knew that Gaels and anglophones fought as both Jacobites and Hanoverians. A number of terms appear in the account for the specific groups involved in the conflict, including *Na Saighdearan Dearga* ("The Red-coat Soldiers"), *An t-Arm Dearg* ("The Red-coat Army"), *Sasannaich* ("English people"), *Goill* ("non-Gaels, Lowlanders"), and *Gàidheil* ("Highlanders"). Even though actual ethnic identity did not align with political allegiance, the text sometimes makes a simple equation between Gaels and the Jacobite cause, on the one hand, and the English and the Hanoverian authorities, on the other, especially in the crescendo of bloodshed on the battlefield of Culloden:

> *Bha 'bhuaidh iomlan air taobh nan Sasannach. Ach gu cinnteach b' iadsan a chaill bu chliùitiche agus bu treuna fhuair na 'bhuidheann a bhuinig; bha dà Shasannach mu'n aon fhear dhe na Gàidheil, bha 'ghaoth leò agus iomadaidh gunna mór a' frasadh nam mìle peilear am-measg nan Gàidheal ...*

> The English side had the complete victory. But certainly, those who lost were more renowned and braver than the side that won; there were two Englishmen for every one of the Gaels, the wind was on their side and many big guns were showering thousands of bullets into the Gaels ...

Not all people from England have been hostile to Gaelic or detrimental to its survival. Like Claire Randall, some have fallen in love with the language and culture after coming to the Highlands and have devoted themselves to learning it and defending it. One of the most important Gaelic lexical resources of the modern era - the Gaelic-to-English dictionary compiled by Edward Dwelly - was the solo effort of a passionately dedicated Englishman. Such are the ironies and contradictions of minoritized languages.

Mac

There may be no word of Gaelic origin in wider circulation than "mac," given that it is contained in the surnames of millions of people around the world: MacDonald, MacKenzie, MacLean, Macintyre, MacQuarrie, MacKay, and so on. It is also in the names of products and companies that have become ubiquitous, from MacDonald's fast-food chain and their menu lineup, such as the "Big Mac," "Egg McMuffin" and "McRib," to Apple's Macintosh computer.

Mac is a Gaelic word meaning "son" and was used to formulate surnames based on the founder of lineages between the twelfth and sixteenth centuries. Before the seventeenth century, surnames were seldom used by anyone but the Highland nobility in order to indicate their membership in particular ruling lineages. The increasing intrusion of the central government in the Highlands, and its mandate to create a bureaucracy with an accountable paper-trail, brought about the imposition of surnames of the sort used in the anglophone world. Church ministers and estate clerks were most often responsible for assigning names to people who appeared in official documents, some of which are considerably different from how the people referred to themselves. The results are a muddle, so much so that one of the great Highland scholars of the twentieth century lamented:

> Surnames of the present day can be unreliable, and even misleading, as evidence of family origins. ... The resulting loss of historical and genealogical identity has been deplorable - a break with the past that can never be fully repaired.

Regardless of internal inconsistencies, Mac-based surnames were such a marker of Gaelic identity that during the sixteenth and seventeenth centuries that anglophones often referred to Gaels, especially in Ireland, as the "Os and Macs."

In early twentieth-century America, "mac" became a slang term used when speaking to a stranger who was male. William Safire, in an essay about how vernacular language reflects regionally-specific social norms and etiquette, wrote in 1984:

> Hey, Mac and hey, buddy are terms most often heard in the Northeast, modifying the imperious hey with a friendly, neutral name. Good buddy is trucker's lingo used by CB'ers. My own preference has been Hey, Mac, perhaps reflecting my own regional background; Jesse Hackell of New City, N.Y., reports using it as in "Hey, Mac, how come you didn't come out to sell me gas when the whatchamacallit went ding?"

Surnames beginning with Mac- would be even more prevalent if Gaels hadn't felt pressure for centuries to eliminate the element from their names. Gaels suffered prejudice and hostility from anglophones in England as well as in Lowland Scotland, and given that the Mac- prefix was a tip-off of a person's Gaelic roots, emigrants often removed it from their names. The Reverend John MacRa graduated from the University of Aberdeen in 1667 and described exactly this practice in his history of the MacRaes, written before his death in 1704:

The name here is spelled MacRa, but varies by the region where any of the clan generally reside. There are various ways of spelling this name: thus in Ireland, they use MacRath and Macgrath; in the north of Scotland, MacRah, MacRae, MacCraw and MacCrow. In England and the south of Scotland, the Mac is left out from an ill-founded prejudice, and the name Rae, Craw, Crow, and such like, are of the same stock.

A whole host of distorted forms arose from this strategy, especially after Gaelic surnames assumed anglophone forms: *MacÙisdein* became "Kitchen," *MacBheathain* ("MacBain") became "Bean," *MacGilleEathain* ("MacLean") became "Clean," *MacGilleFhionntain* became "Clinton," and so on.

Another trick was to replace the Mac- prefix with a "-son" suffix so that *MacDhomhnaill* became "Donaldson," *MacFhearchair* became "Farquharson," *MacFhearghuis* became "Fergusson," *MacMhathain* became "Matheson," and so on. A more extreme measure was to simply replace the Gaelic surname with an anglophone one that bore some vague resemblance to it: *MacEachairn* ("MacEachern") was replaced by "Cochrane," *Mac an Oighre* ("MacNair") became "Wier," *MacDhunléibhe* became "Livingston," and so on.

Mac- surnames usually dominated among Highland emigrants who settled overseas colonies, and their names have become the most enduring marker of their Gaelic origins. The town of Maxton in North Carolina was named for the predominance of Mac- surnames, as was the town of Maxville in Ontario.

Oscar

The Academy Awards grants trophies, referred to colloquially as "Oscars," every year to recognize and reward exceptional achievements in the cinematic arts. The trophy is a small statue in the Art Deco style in the shape of a knight and has been rewarded in an annual ceremony every year since 1929. The trophies began to be referred to officially as "Oscars" in 1939, although there is disagreement about why, when, and how the name came to designate this award.

The name "Oscar" can be found in many parts of the world today. Oscar Meyer (1859-1955) immigrated from Württemberg (which became part of Germany) to Detroit in 1873 and founded a processed-meat company that produces a highly popular sausage that bears his name.

The name "Oscar" was popularized in Latin America through the prominence of the Brazilian architect Oscar Niemeyer (1907-2012) and the human rights champion Óscar Romero of El Salvador (1917-1980) who was beatified in 2015.

Oscar is originally a Gaelic name that means "lover of deer." A character named "Oscar" (usually spelled "Osgar" in modern Scottish Gaelic) began to appear in the Fenian cycle of Gaelic legends in the eleventh century as the grandson of the warrior-poet Fionn MacCumhaill. Oscar was the strongman of the war-band commanded by Fionn called the *Fian* (also called in English the "Fianna," or "Fenians"). He served as a symbol of brawn in Gaelic literature for centuries. Eòin Dubh, the chieftain of the MacGregors who died in 1519, for example, was praised by his poet as having *Lámh mar Osgar is gach cath* "A hand like Oscar in every battle."

The Fenian cycle is a set of inter-related stories centered on the Fian, who were the protectors and defenders of the Gaelic world of Scotland and Ireland against the invading Vikings and other hostile enemies. The cycle is similar in many ways to the tales of Arthur's knights of the Round Table. This corpus of material survives both in manuscript from the medieval period and in oral tradition and belongs equally to Ireland and Gaelic Scotland.

In 1760 James Macpherson, a young Highlander from Badenoch, anonymously published *Fragments of Ancient Poetry, Collected in the Highlands of Scotland, and translated from the Galic or Erse language.* Macpherson took certain elements from the Gaelic ballads about the Fian – characters, themes, plot-lines – but reworked them considerably in new forms to meet the aesthetic expectations of his anglophone audience.

Rather than admitting to the degree to which he had reworked the tales, however, he claimed that the epic poetry in this and later volumes was a literal translation of the Gaelic verse of the legendary poet Oisean, the son of Fionn MacCumhaill and father of Oscar. Macpherson renamed him "Ossian" and the series of books that Macpherson wrote are usually referred to collectively as *Ossian*.

Macpherson enjoyed success beyond his wildest dreams. The poetry and sentiments of *Ossian* stirred the hearts of poets and scholars across Europe and America, from Wordsworth and Blake to Goethe,

Tennyson, and Thomas Jefferson. It was literally the seed from which the European Romantic Movement was born.

Napoleon Bonaparte carried a copy of *Ossian* in his breast pocket and commissioned Jean Auguste Dominique Ingres to paint a colossal scene from the epic in his palace. Jean Bernadotte of France (1763-1844), who was a Marshal of France under Napoleon, became King Charles XIV John of Sweden and Norway in 1818. His son, who succeeded him as king of Sweden and Norway in 1844, was given the name "Oscar" by Napoleon himself. This was how the name "Oscar" was introduced into Scandinavia and from there into other parts of modern Europe.

It is perhaps fitting that a name with an international appeal associated with heroic storytelling should adorn these renowned awards. It would also be fitting for more people to recognize its Gaelic pedigree.

Community
and Customs

Clan

"Clan" is a common word in English used to describe kin-based societies. It was used in anglophone sources of the Lowlands from the fifteenth century onwards in reference to the social groups of the Highlands, but then subsequently applied to other societies perceived to be "tribal," such as the ancient Romans, the Arabs, and the native inhabitants of the Americas. It has also been adopted into the terminology used by anglophone anthropologists, biologists, and geologists.

"Clan" was, of course, employed extensively in the poetry and fiction of Walter Scott and others who described traditional life in the Scottish Highlands. From the 1820 poetic epic *Yamoyden: A Tale of the Wars of King Philip* to Jean Auel's 1980 *The Clan of the Cave Bear*, the noun "clan" has been used in literature that portrays societies, real and imagined, presumed to be primitive.

The fact that this word was borrowed from Gaelic into Lowland Scots in the sixteenth century and then into English in the seventeenth century to describe kin-based societies suggests that anglophones perceived themselves to live according to a different organizing principle, and that they thus needed to acquire a suitable word from another group who they perceived as living in a more primitive social structure. Gaelic *clann* provided such a word for anglophones in the early modern period.

Many different words have been used for kin-groups in Gaelic: *clann* was actually borrowed from the Brythonic or British Latin word *planta*, meaning "children." The term began to be used to signify kin-groups in Ireland in the tenth century, and had become the dominant term in Scotland by the twelfth century. This is when Highland clans, as we know them now, began to emerge as a hybrid of Gaelic kin-based society and the Anglo-Norman feudal settlement in Scotland, and the first names of clans began to be coined. In the sixteenth century, however, *cinneadh* began to replace *clann* as the preferred term in Gaelic.

Clans were not made up solely of extended families related by blood, but were instead social groups led by a dominant ruling family and united by a variety of social bonds. The clan would be named after the founder of that dynasty, but as branches of descendants split off and vied for power, clans could go in and out of existence. The first recorded clan names in Scotland, Clann Chanann and Clann Morgainn, were written into the eleventh-century notes in the *Book of Deer* in the north-east of Scotland, but never again appear in the annals of history.

The way in which clan names are used in English often deviate significantly from their original forms in Gaelic: anglophones often refer to "Clan MacDonald," for example, but "Clan Donald" corresponds more accurately to the actual name *Clann Domhnaill*. Some of these distortions are the results of mangled anglicizations of Gaelic surnames. The MacKinnons are known in Gaelic as *Clann Fhionghain*, the MacLeans as *Clann Ghill-Eathain*, and the Robertsons as *Clann Donnchaidh*, for example.

The major dynasties in the Highlands founded by Anglo-Normans were not given kin names using *clann* in Gaelic, but are designated more generically: *Na Cuimeinich* "The Cummings," *Na Frisealaich* "The Frasers," *Na Granndaich* "The Grants," *Na Siosalaich* "The Chisholms," and *Na Stiùbhartaich* "The Stewarts."

The most infamous use of the word "clan" is that used in the name of a secret society formed in Pulaski, Tennessee, in 1866 by six Confederate soldiers who used violence, and the threat of violence, to enforce white supremacy in the American South: the Ku Klux Klan. The founders chose titles and symbolism from an eclectic mix of influences - fraternal orders such as the Masons, Greek mythology, Biblical stories, fairy tales - but there is no evidence that they themselves had any direct knowledge of Highland heritage. When such imagery - such as the fiery cross - was co-opted by these peddlers of racism and hate, they did so via imaginative literature in English, especially that written by Walter Scott.

The word "clan" has continued to be used in the names of groups and gangs in popular anglophone culture, from the Clan McDuck - from whom the Disney character Scrooge McDuck is supposed to descend - to the hip-hop artists Wu-Tang Clan.

The Highland clan system had already been weakened before the defeat of the Jacobite forces at the Battle of Culloden in 1746 triggered the sweeping away of the last of the old aristocracy willing to uphold Gaelic ideals. The clans as fully functioning social units were made obsolete along with them. Since then, various words, names, tokens, and customs derived from Highland clan life have fed the imaginations and aspirations of those who are attracted by the idea of a rural, kin-based society rooted in the ancient Scottish past. As Walter Scott might have said, "The clan is dead, long live the clan!"

Slogan

Nowadays, most people think of a slogan as a pithy catchphrase or motto used to promote the identity of corporations or their products. Nike advertises its brand of shoes, for example, with the slogan "Just Do It" and Apple its vast line of gadgets with "Think Different."

"Slogan" came to be used commonly in the anglophone world to refer to group mottos in the 1880s. In her book *Odd or Even?*, for example, published in 1880, the American author Adeline Whitney essentially equates slogan and motto in a religious context: " 'Duty, God, immortality,' the very slogan of the pulpit, these were getting to be as dead words as the motto of the French Republic." Businessmen caught on to the handy word by the 1920s, as demonstrated by an article in the American periodical *Publishers Weekly* in 1928: "As an advertising man, Mr. Calkins believes the slogan 'a cent a copy to sell the art of reading', a great and revolutionary one."

The term "slogan" is derived from the Gaelic term *sluagh-ghairm*, which can be translated as "war-band-exclamation." The slogan was usually the name of a place where warriors would muster in the case of an emergency. Each clan had its own gathering place where the battle host would meet, so each clan had its own unique slogan.

William Buchanan provided one of the first descriptions of the practice by a native Scottish Gael, recorded no later than 1723:

> The isle of Clàr Innis was the *sluagh-ghairm* proper to the family of Buchanan; such like being usual in all other families in these times and for some following ages. So soon as this call was raised upon any alarm, the word *Clàr Innis* was sounded aloud from one to another, in a very little time, throughout the whole country; upon hearing of which all effective men belonging to the laird of Buchanan with the utmost diligence repaired well armed to the ordinary place of rendezvous which, when the lairds resided in that island, was upon a ground on the opposite shore.

Writers in the Scottish Lowlands began remarking on this Highland practice in the sixteenth century, rendering the Gaelic word with spellings such as slogorne, sloghorne and slughorne. Although there are scattered references to the *sluagh-ghairm* in antiquarian texts, it was the fiction of Walter Scott that brought the word to the attention of a large English-speaking audience. Scott used "slogan" in a number of his works, including *Minstrelsy of the Scottish Border* (1802), *The Lay of the Last Minstrel* (1805) and *Marmion* (1808).

Other nineteenth-century writers, such as Jane Porter, took up the term "slogan," as well as related words and ideas from the Highland clan system to add impact to their imaginative literature set in Scotland of old.

Another example of an archaic symbol co-opted into anglophone literature is the so-called "fiery cross." In Gaelic this was actually a charred stick, not a flaming firebrand, simply called the *crois-tàraidh* "summoning-cross" or *crann-tàra* "summoning-stick." This sign of crisis was rushed from village to village and used along with the *sluagh-ghairm* to compel clansfolk to meet at the designated gathering place. The Ku Klux Klan took this symbol from the 1905 novel *The Clansman* by the American author Thomas Dixon, who in turn took the image from the fiction of Walter Scott. The Klan interpreted the English name of the practice literally, setting a wooden cross ablaze and using it to terrorize people with the threat of racist violence. This borrowing must be seen as an example of cultural appropriation via literature rather than a living tradition with any continuity within the same community.

Historical details frequently give way to striking images that germinate in the fertile imaginations of storytellers. Some people would argue that advertisers are among the most influential storytellers of our time, but it is not always wise to follow such simplistic slogans as "Just Do It."

Cairn

A "cairn" is a pile of stones, sometimes arranged neatly to form a stable structure or sometimes to create the impression of a megalithic ruin. Cairns are generally understood to commemorate the ancestral dead in one way or another. The Gaelic term *carn* was borrowed into Lowland Scots by the sixteenth century, or was at least familiar to Scots speakers, given that William Stewart (c. 1476 – c. 1548) used it in his translation of the Latin history of Scotland originally written by Hector Boece. The word also appears in a "flyting" (poetic duel) by Lowland poet Alexander Montgomerie about the year 1600. As you may have come to expect, the word "cairn" also appears in the works of Robert Burns and Walter Scott as well around the turn of the nineteenth century.

One of the most iconic cairns in the Highlands was built in 1881 in the shape of a tower twenty feet high at Culloden, commemorating the battle fought there on 16 April 1746. A replica of this cairn was built in Knoydart, Nova Scotia, in 1938, near the graves of three soldiers who had fought at the Battle of Culloden and emigrated later to Canada. The cairn has become a common form of memorializing Highland emigrants and their emigrant legacy in many parts of the world.

The original Gaelic word, *carn*, is used in hundreds of place names across Scotland. The most mammoth instance is the Cairngorms mountain range in the eastern Highlands - although this name was not actually created by Gaelic speakers or natives of the region. It seems to have been invented by Colonel Thomas Thornton, an Englishman who toured the area and published memoirs of his tour in 1804. The native name for the mountain range in *Am Monadh Ruadh* "The Red Mountain." Although *monadh* is a commonplace word in modern Scottish Gaelic, it was a medieval borrowing from Pictish.

Probably the earliest surviving explanation of the significance of the *carn* is from an Old Gaelic tale composed in the eighth or ninth century called *Togail bruidne Dá Derga* "The destruction of Dá Derga's hostel." The narrator of the story actually digresses for a moment to describe these monuments:

> For two causes they built their cairns: first, since this was a custom in marauding; and, secondly, that they might find out their losses at the

Hostel. Every one that would come safe from it would take his stone from the cairn: thus the stones of those that were slain would be left, and by that they would know their losses.

In other words, before a battle, every warrior would place a stone in the heap. If they returned from the battle alive, they would remove a stone from the pile. The body count thus corresponded to the number of stones left in the cairn; a tall cairn signifies a tremendous loss of life.

THE BATTLE
OF CULLODEN
WAS FOUGHT ON THIS MOOR
16TH APRIL 1746.
THE GRAVES OF THE
GALLANT HIGHLANDERS
WHO FOUGHT FOR
SCOTLAND & PRINCE CHARLIE
ARE MARKED BY THE NAMES
OF THEIR CLANS.

Some Gaelic medieval texts reflect the same practice, but later Scottish texts also suggest that some cairns were raised to commemorate the death of a single person. An anonymous Highland source writing c.1685 suggests that these memorials could serve to fuel the animosities of feuds:

To keep up the Feuds they erect a Cairn of Stones in the place where their Friend was killed, calling it by his name. There also they draw deep Crosse there so they may be kept in mynde to be reveng'd.

Martin Martin, a native Gaelic speaker from the Isle of Skye, recorded the use of cairns in the late seventeenth century in association with religious pilgrimages in certain areas, especially where Catholicism still prevailed:

There are many Cairns, or Heaps of Stones in this Island. Some of the Natives say they were erected in the times of Heathenism, and that the antient Inhabitants worship'd about them. In Popish Countries, the People still retain the antient Custom of making a Tour around them.

Others say, these Cairns were erected where Persons of Distinction, kill'd in Battle, had been bury'd, and that their Urns were laid in the ground under the Cairns. ...

There are little Cairns to be seen in some places on the common Road, which were made only where Corps happen'd to rest for some minutes; but they have laid aside the making (of) such Cairns now.

Cairns were created and used in the Scottish Highlands in numerous ways associated with the dead. They were regarded with special deference and reverence, which is the attitude that most cultures hold toward their ancestors. In fact, Edmund Burt, an English officer stationed in the Highlands in the 1720s who wrote a series of letters to a correspondent in London, remarked in wonder at the veneration that Highlanders showed for these piles of rocks and the taboos that kept them from desecrating them:

I have made mention of their funeral piles in a formal letter; but I had once occasion to take particular notice of a heap of stones, near the middle of a small piece of arable land. The plough was carefully guided as near to it as possible; and the pile, being like others I had seen upon the moors, I asked, by an interpreter, whether there was a rock beneath it; but being answered in the negative, I further inquired the reasons why they lost so much ground, and did not remove the heap. To this I had an answer, it was a burial place, and they deemed it a kind of sacrilege to remove a single stone; and that the children from their infancy, were taught the same veneration for it. Thus a parcel of loose stones are more religiously preserved among them than, with us, the costly monuments in Westminster Abbey; and thence I could not but conclude that the inclination to preserve the remains and memory of the dead is greater with those people than it is among us.

Although the word *carn* is found in all of the surviving Celtic languages of western Europe, it has been argued that it was not inherited from the Indo-European family. If this argument is correct, *carn* may actually be one of the few words inherited from the ancient people who lived along the Atlantic seaboard during the Age of Megaliths before the coming, or emergence, of Celtic languages in the region. That is a testimony to the long memories of Celtic peoples, their resilience, their adherence to tradition, and the power of words.

Bard

The noun "bard," referring to an upscale poet, has a long history in the English language. The English dramatist and poet William Shakespeare is probably most commonly associated with the word, although the computer game *The Bard's Tale*, which has had numerous incarnations since the 1980s, has brought it to the attention of millions of young people through digital media.

Poets have been held in very high esteem in Celtic societies from our earliest records, attesting to the cultural value invested in literature and the power of the word in political, religious, and social settings. One of the first writers to comment on the bard as a member of the élite professions of Celtic society was Diodorus Siculus, a Greek historian who compiled the volume *The Library of History* between about 60 BC and 40 BC from the work of previous scholars. He testifies:

> They have lyric poets called Bards, who, accompanied by instruments resembling lyres, sing both praise and satire. ... Not only during peacetime but also in war, the Gauls obey with great care these Druids and singing poets, both friend and enemy alike.

The Greek writer Athenæus compiled a book on dining customs late in the second century AD drawing from earlier texts, providing further interesting details about the ancient Celtic bards from sources that have since been lost:

> Posidonius, in the twenty-third book of his *Histories*, says that the Celts have with them, even in war, companions whom they call *parasites* "those who dine at another's table." These poets recite their praises in large companies and crowds, and before each of the listeners according to rank. Their tales are recounted by those called Bards, poets who recite praises in song.

Forms of the word "bard" have survived in all of the modern Celtic languages, again demonstrating the central role that poets and poetry have played in Celtic societies for millennia. The word has thus entered English from multiple points of contact with Celtic-speaking peoples although it has its own distinct history within Scotland.

The duties of the bard and the nature of their poetic craft have changed significantly over time. It seems that when Gaels converted to Christianity in the early medieval period, the range of roles and privileges of the poets were expanded to fill the vacuum left by the banishing of druids. The former pagan holy men reserved the most important aspects of the literary profession for themselves, calling themselves *filid* (singular *fili*) "seers." Although there were constant adjustments, this essential hierarchy, with the *filid* on top and the bards below, was enshrined in the Gaelic institutions of learning throughout the medieval period.

The formal institutions of Gaelic learning were much more numerous and entrenched in Ireland than in Scotland, so there was more social fluidity in the Highlands. As the history of the Campbells of Craignish relates in about the year 1720, many chieftains employed the lower-order bard to fulfill multiple roles.

> Every considerable family in the Highlands had their Bards & Shenachies. The Bard was the Family poet, & the Shenachie their prose wryter, but very oft the Bard supply'd the place of both. These Offices were heretable, & had a pension, commonly a piece of land annexed to that Office. Their work was to hand down to posterity the valorous actions, Conquests, batles, skirmishes, marriages, relations of the predicessors, by repeating & singing the same at births, baptisms, marriages, feasts and funeralls, so that no people since the Curse of the Almighty dissipated the Jews took such care to keep their Tribes, Cadets and branches, so well & so distinctly separate.

Their counterparts in the Scottish Lowlands, however, did not always hold Gaelic versifiers in such high regard. Some of the earliest appearances of "bard" in Lowland documents relate to efforts to regulate or abolish wandering Gaelic minstrels and other itinerants that the authorities saw as disorderly or a burden on the population. An Act of the Scottish Parliament in 1449, for example, says that enforcers should "inquere at ilk courte gif thar be ony that makis thaim fulis that ar nocht, bardis, or sic lik utheris rynnaris aboute" ("inquire at each court if there be any that make them fools that are not, bards, or such like other runners-about"). In 1562 the Synod of Aberdeen passed a resolution that "all commoun skoldis, flyttaris, and bardis to be baneist the toun" ("all common storytellers, dueling-versifiers, and bards to be banished from the town").

Despite these prohibitions and the attack on Gaelic literary tradition in general, the figure of the bard has been an enduring one in the Scottish Highlands and the immigrant communities where oral tradition has survived. In fact, it would not be an exaggeration to say that poets have been some of the greatest tradition-bearers and culture-heroes in the Gaelic world, defending the integrity and validity of their native language and heritage.

Many of the Gaelic poets of greatest renown have been known by nicknames containing the word *bard*. To name just a few with whom most Gaelic speakers in the present will be familiar: *Am Bard MacGillEathain* ("The Bard MacLean," John MacLean of Tiree and Nova Scotia 1787-1848), *Bard Loch Fine* ("The Bard of Lochfyne," Evan MacColl of Lochfyneside in Argyll and Toronto 1808-98), and *Bard Mhealaboist* ("The Bard of Melbost," Murdo MacFarlane 1901-82).

While the term "bard" may have an archaic, esoteric or pretentious ring to it in English, it is a central pillar and organizing principle in the Scottish Gaelic world to the present day.

Gillie, Ghillie

Hunting and fishing in the Scottish Highlands have become past-times reserved for the wealthy who typically hire a "gillie," or man-servant, on these expeditions. The gillie typically carries equipment, guides the hunters or fishers through the landscape, helps to locate the wild-life, and lugs the haul back to their lodgings. The term "gillie" or "ghillie" began to be used in this sense in Lowland Scottish texts from the 1830s. The Scottish Country Sports Tourism Group, promoting this activity commercially, go so far as to claim on their website:

> At the sharp end of sport in Scotland are an exceptional group of men who have the experience of centuries behind them. Generations within families have followed the footsteps of those before to deliver sport to visitors from every country across the globe. They are men of the land, taking pride in what they do to the highest level, always seeking to give the utmost experience to the visitor in a way that is befitting of such an historic sporting nation.

This word will also be familiar those who participate in the many branches of Scottish dance tradition. The dance *Gille Chaluim* "Malcolm's Servant," often anglicized as "Gille Callum," and sometimes simply called "the Sword Dance," is a popular one in Highland Dancing. The dance demonstrates the agility of the dancer in leaping around the blades of two crossed swords. It is first mentioned by this name in 1804, although a tune by this name, meant for dancing, was published in a collection between 1730 and 1765.

Since the 1930s the standard footwear for people participating in Scottish Highland Dancing and Scottish Country Dancing has been soft shoes made of supple leather called "ghillies." They have also become widely adopted by female Irish dancers.

These terms are borrowings of the Gaelic noun *gille*, meaning "young man, servant." In the early medieval period it referred most specifically to a male who had reached the age to bear arms, although it could include the range of roles that a young man could take, such as pupil, servant or messenger.

There is a slew of Highland surnames that have the element *gille* in them. These began to be used in about the tenth century and indicated devotion to a particular saint. Monks also went by names of this form and because they were not celibate in medieval Gaeldom and in fact often founded dynasties that monopolized church power, their devotional titles were inherited by their children. These names were sometimes also given to children because they were born on the feast day of a saint.

Original Gaelic Surname	Meaning	Anglicized
MacGilleBrìde	"Son of the servant of Bridget"	Gilbride, Gilbert, MacBride
MacGilleChrìosta	"Son of the servant of Christ"	Gilchrist
MacGilleÌosa	"Son of the servant of Jesus"	Gillies, MacLeish
MacGilleFhaolain	"Son of the servant of Faolan"	MacLellan, MacLelland
MacGilleFhinnein	"Son of the servant of Finnan"	MacLennan
MacGilleMhìcheil	"Son of the servant of Michael"	Carmichael
MacGilleMoire	"Son of the servant of Mary"	Gilmore
MacGilleEathain	"Son of the servant of John"	MacLean, MacLane

Highland chieftains were always accompanied by a retinue of attendants, each of which had his own title and duty. A partial list of these, many of which contain *gille* in their titles, was provided by the English officer Edmund Burt, stationed in the Highlands in the 1720s:

Bard (Chieftain's poet)
Bleideir (Chieftain's spokesman)
Gille Mór (Chieftain's broadsword keeper)
Gille Cas fhliuch (Carries chieftain over wet and boggy terrain)
Gille Comh-sreathainn (Leads chieftain's horse in rough ground)
Gille Truis-àirnis (Carries chieftain's possessions)
Pìobaire (Bagpiper)
Gille a' Phìobaire (Bagpiper's servant)

Gille is also just the common Gaelic word for a son or adult male, like modern Lowland Scots "lad."

Coronach

The noun "coronach" refers to the traditional communal lamentation of death, or the sounds of wailing and shouting that occurred at such ceremonies. It began appearing in Lowland Scots literature in the sixteenth century, such as when William Dunbar characterized Highlanders in his poem "The Dance of the Seven Deadly Sins" by the din they made during the rituals of death: "Be he the correnoch had done schout."

Several different eighteenth-century accounts of the Highlands provide descriptions – usually brief and impressionistic – of the coronach as an aspect of the rites of passage of death. Edmund Burt, an Englishman stationed in the Highlands in the 1720s, describes it in very unflattering terms:

> The upper-class women hire women to moan and lament at the funeral of their nearest relations. These women cover their heads with a small piece of cloth, mostly green, and every now and then break out into a hideous howl and 'Ho-bo-bo-bo-boo', as I have often heard is done in some parts of Ireland. This part of the ceremony is called 'coronach' ...

Lowlanders and other anglophones saw this custom as alien to their own social norms, exemplifying the barbarity and irrationality of the Highlanders. By the late eighteenth century, like so many other cultural markers, the coronach became part of the stock literary imagery used by anglophone authors to represent and highlight Highland distinctiveness. Walter Scott composed his first original poem in 1798 and titled it "Glenfinlas; or, Lord Ronald's Coronach." It was an early literary experiment, however, and did not earn him many accolades.

Scott's reputation as a poet crested with the publication of *The Lady of the Lake* in 1810. This tale in verse is set in the southern Highlands and consists of six different sections, or "Cantos." A portion of one of these is called "Coronach," and is based loosely on a traditional Gaelic lament.

Alexander Scott (1920-1989) fought with the Gordon Highlanders during the Second World War and took part in the Normandy landings. He later became the first head of the department of Scottish Literature at the University of Glasgow. His poem "Coronach" is a lament to the dead soldiers of the Gordon Highlanders and a meditation on the responsibilities of the poet to speak to the living for the dead. It is both melancholy and eerie.

Waement the deid I never did,
But nou I am safe awa
I hear their wae
Greetan greetan dark and daw -
Their wierd to sing, my wierd to dae.

The idea of the coronach has continued to inform the way that people think about Highland tradition, especially given that modernity has generally made it more difficult to express and process deep grief and the social rituals associated with mourning. In this sense, the coronach represents a lost past that some people would like to recover. The coronach ritual is mentioned in the *Outlander* series and an historical romance novel called *Coronach* was published in 2007.

"Coronach" is a borrowing of the Gaelic compound *comh-rànach* meaning "crying together." It is somewhat ironic that the English form of the word can be found more often in anglophone texts than the original form can be found in Gaelic texts.

There are at least two reasons for the scarcity of *comhranach* in Gaelic texts. First of all, there are other terms for the keen, or funeral lamentation, that became more common in the last few centuries in the Highlands, such as *caoineadh, caoidh, tuiream,* and *tuireadh*. In this sense, the medieval Lowland Scots borrowing is a fossilization of an earlier usage largely lost in modern Gaelic.

On top of that, the church saw the keen as a holdover from paganism and did its best to suppress it. Further disapproval in secular society finally started to have a negative effect in the eighteenth century. Walter Scott himself commented in a footnote to his poem *The Lady of the Lake* that it was going extinct, and writes about it in the past tense:

> The Coronach of the Highlanders, like the Ululatus of the Romans, and the Ululoo of the Irish, was a wild expression of lamentation, poured forth by the mourners over the body of a departed friend. When the words of it were articulate, they expressed the praises of the deceased, and the loss the clan would sustain by his death. ... The coronach has for some years past been suspended at funerals by the use of the bagpipe; and that also is, like many other Highland peculiarities, falling into disuse, unless in remote districts.

One of the only early references in Gaelic to the coronach by this name is in a poem written by Niall MacMhuirich, one of the greatest masters of the classical tradition in Scotland, in the second half of the sixteenth century. MacMhuirich composed a biting satire of bagpipers he encountered, claiming a special place in Hell for the instruments and the noise they made:

> *Gur coranaich bhan is pìob-ghleadhair*
> *Dà leannan ciùil cluas nan deomhan.*

> The coronach of women and the roar of pipes
> Are the two darlings of music in the devils' ears.

While it may be that MacMhuirich disliked these particular players of the bagpipe, or that his recent illness made him ill-disposed to hearing such a strident sound, we can also expect that the professional poets of his era were more attuned to the gentler sound of the harp that accompanied their public performances and looked askance at the upstart instrument.

Other than this remote and obscure reference, however, the term *comhranach* (or variant forms like *coranach*) is scarcely to be seen in the extensive Gaelic literature that survives. Perhaps that is a loss that has yet to be properly lamented.

Beltane

Beltane is a name for the ancient Celtic calendar day falling around May 1 marking the beginning of the light half of the year. The holiday is recognized and celebrated in different communities with Celtic heritage in many different ways, from small and humble to grandiose. The Beltane Fire Society has been staging huge theatrical performances on Calton Hill in Edinburgh since 1988, drawing large crowds and media attention but veering wildly off script from the traditional folk customs that have been in continuous practice for many centuries.

Beltane occupies a special place in the annual calendar and is tuned to the rhythms of the pastoral economy, so it is not surprising that the word began to be recorded in Lowland Scots legal documents in the early fifteenth century. As one of the major quarter days in Gaelic tradition, it was a convenient means of subdividing the year for practical purposes, especially as it indicated the arrival of mild weather. By the later sixteenth century, a range of folk customs in Lowland Scotland were being drawn to the observance of Beltane, including bonfires, folk dramas, and pilgrimages to healing wells.

Beltane was borrowed even earlier into the English of Lancashire. The term "Beltancu" appears in documents from the twelfth century referring to rents paid in the form of cattle every three years on May day, a practice surviving from the Brythonic peoples who lived in the region before the Anglo-Saxon invasions. Yet the word "Beltan" itself was grafted onto the financial transactions by Gaelic speakers who settled the region in the early tenth century from the communities founded earlier by the Norse around the Irish Sea, including the Western Isles of Scotland. There could hardly be a better example than this of the convoluted cultural exchanges between the ethnic groups and languages in the British Isles, one in which Gaelic has left its own mark.

Antiquarians and local historians of the eighteenth and nineteenth century recorded many ways in which Beltane was celebrated, and writers of historical fiction have drawn on these accounts to transport their readers to the colorful spectacles of the past. Walter Scott's first original poem "Glenfinlas; or, Lord Ronald's Coronach," for example, composed in 1798, refers to Beltane, as does Lord Byron's first volume of poetry, *Hours of Idleness*, published in 1807. In the popular historical romance *Outlander*, the heroine Claire has her fateful encounter at the standing stones on Beltane.

The name for this festival day occurs in early medieval Gaelic texts and its origin has long caused debate among Celtic etymologists, but it is likely to have meant "bright fire" or "fire-gap" to those who coined it. *Cormac's Glossary*, written in about the year 900, provides a speculative derivation of the word that nonetheless describes the lighting of bonfires for the purification of livestock that continued into the modern era in both Ireland and Gaelic Scotland: "Beltane, that is Bel's fire, that is the fire of Bel, that is two auspicious fires the druids made with great spells and each year they brought the cattle between them against pestilence."

John Ramsay of Ochtertyre, drawing from the memories of older Highlanders, recorded particularly interesting accounts in the late eighteenth century:

> But the most considerable of the Druidical festivals is that of Beltane, or May-day, which was lately observed in some parts of the Highlands with extraordinary ceremonies. Of later years it is chiefly attended to by young people, persons advanced in years considering it as inconsistent with their gravity to give it any countenance. Yet a number of circumstances relative to it may be collected from tradition, or the conversation of very old people, who witnessed this feast in their youth, when the ancient rites were better observed. ...
>
> Thither the young folks repaired in the morning, and cut a trench, on the summit of which a seat of turf was formed for the company. And in the middle a pile of wood or other fuel was placed, which of old they kindled with *tein'-éiginn* - i.e., forced-fire or need-fire. Although, for many years past, they have been contented with common fire, yet we shall now describe the process, because it will hereafter appear that recourse is still had to the *tein'-éiginn* upon extraordinary emergencies.
>
> The night before, all the fires in the country were carefully extinguished, and next morning the materials for exciting this sacred fire were prepared. The most primitive method seems to be that which was used in the islands of Skye, Mull, and Tiree. A well-seasoned plank of oak was procured, in the midst of which a hole was bored. A wimble of the same timber was then applied, the end of which they fitted to the hole. But in some parts of the mainland the machinery was different. They used a frame of green wood, of a square form, in the centre of which was an axle-tree. In some places three times three persons, in others three times nine, were required for turning round by turns the axle-tree or wimble. If any of them had been guilty of murder, adultery, theft, or other atrocious crime, it was imagined either that the fire would not kindle, or that it would be devoid of its usual virtue. So soon as any sparks were emitted by means of the violent friction, they applied a species of agaric which grows on old birch-trees, and is very combustible. This fire had the appearance of being immediately derived from heaven, and manifold were the virtues ascribed to it. They esteemed it a preservative against witch-craft, and a sovereign remedy against malignant diseases, both in the human species and in cattle; and by it the strongest poisons were supposed to have their nature changed. ...
>
> This festival was longest observed in the interior Highlands, for towards the west coast the traces of it are faintest. ... It is probable that at the original

Beltane festival there were two fires kindled near one another. When any person is in a critical dilemma, pressed on each side by unsurmountable difficulties, the Highlanders have a proverb: *Tha e eadar an dà theine Bealltainn* "He is between the two Beltane fires."

The lighting of these ritual fires on hills and summits was such an ardent and established tradition in Gaelic Scotland that there are places whose name includes Beltane in them. Tullybelton, north-west of Perth, is derived from *Tulaich Bhealltainn* "the Hill of Beltane" and was first recorded with this name in 1369.

Fire is not the only element prominent in the traditional Gaelic celebrations of Beltane, however. The ritual of washing one's face in the morning dew has survived to the present, and in the past, pilgrimages to local holy wells was a common practice, especially for those in need of healing.

It is fair to say that Beltane has left a profound mark on the landscape, on the ritual calendar, and on the cultural imagination of Scotland, and on those for whom the heritage of the Highlands burns bright.

Banshee

The banshee is a supernatural figure that is widespread in modern folklore, as well as in literature in genres such as horror, fantasy, and historical romance. She is a female wraith, closely associated with aristocratic families, whose deaths she mourns or forewarns: hence the common expression "wailing like a banshee." The banshee is well represented in popular anglophone culture, used as the names of a television series, a Marvel comic book character, and a rock band (Siouxsie and the Banshees), just to name a few examples.

Nowadays the banshee is assumed to be a specifically Irish figure, but she is actually an element of pan-Gaelic cosmology shared across Scotland and Ireland. Not only that, but the word actually first came into English from Gaelic via Scotland in the eighteenth century, even if its Irish associations became dominant later.

Its first appearance in print was in the travelogue written by English naturalist Thomas Pennant about his 1769 tour of Scotland, printed in 1771, in which he observed, "The death of people is supposed to be foretold by the cries and shrieks of *Benshi*, or the Fairies wife, uttered along the very path where the funeral is to pass." Walter Scott also picked up on Gaelic beliefs about death omens in his celebrated poem *The Lady of the Lake*, published in 1810, in which he invokes "the fatal Ben-Shie's boding scream." The ominous apparition was soon to be found in other works of anglophone literature set in the Gaelic world, whether of Scotland or Ireland.

The English form "ben-shi" or "banshee" is a borrowing of Gaelic *ban-sìdh* (or *bean-sìdh*) "female fairy." Stories and beliefs about fairy beings and the Otherworld occupy a central place in Gaelic cosmology and folklore, and scholars have increasingly come to appreciate the complexity and multifaceted nature of this material. It serves many different purposes and takes many different forms, and so cannot be easily generalized. It is also very old: the *sìdhichean*, as they are generally called in modern Scottish Gaelic, are the original pre-Christian pantheon of the Gaels. The term *áes-sídhe* "the people of fairy" was recorded in Gaelic texts by the eighth century for these divine beings who were associated with the *sìdhean* "burial mound, fairy hillock."

Unlike the fairies of modern anglophone tradition, who are generally portrayed as small and winged, most *sìdhichean* in Gaelic tradition are virtually indistinguishable from human beings. Among the most important and powerful of the fairy host is the female who is attached to the ruling dynasty of a clan territory. There are numerous names for these figures in different localities, but they are related to pan-Gaelic beliefs about the territorial goddess of sovereignty to whom the human male leader was symbolically married when he was inaugurated. If he performed his duties and maintained his relationship with the goddess of the territory faithfully, the land and people would flourish. It is this intimate connection between king (or chieftain) and land goddess that moved the *ban-sìdh* to keen with sorrow when he died – or even in anticipation of his death.

The coronach – the keen performed at burials – was understood as having pre-Christian origins, and early medieval texts even credited the goddess Bríg for having invented it. Beliefs in these powerful female land goddesses who gave legitimacy to male leaders also upheld aspects of feminine power and authority in the human world, as well as the importance of the keening tradition and other female-specific customs. The increasing power of the anglophone world and its hostility to Gaelic culture and identity had a negative impact on these beliefs and customs, particularly from the eighteenth century onward.

Although the banshee still continues to appear in Gaelic oral tradition – where it was not stamped out by the aggressive disapproval of church ministers and school teachers –, belief in and fear of her has continually diminished over time. Regardless of past cultural tides, perhaps a resurgence of interest in native Gaelic cosmology and tradition, and a desire to manifest feminine divinity, will sweep her back into power in the future. Just hope that you don't hear her wailing your name in the dark of night ...

Warfare

Claymore

One of the most persistent images associated with the Highland clans is the long sword commonly referred to in English as the "claymore." From *Braveheart* to *Outlander*, and in even earlier works of fiction, the image of the muscular warrior brandishing a massive blade has served to underscore the stereotype of the macho Scottish Highlander on the field of combat.

A single early use of the word "claymore" appears in an account about the Clan Gregor, led by the infamous Rob Roy, in 1715. Sir Humphrey Colquhoun of Luss and James Grant of Pluscarden assembled forces to confront the MacGregors, and the clothing and weaponry of their Highland soldiers are described in detail:

> in their short hose and belted plaids, arm'd each of 'em with a well fix'd gun on his shoulder, a strong handsome target, with a sharp pointed steel, of above half an ell in length, screw'd into the navel of it, on his left arm, a sturdy claymore by his side, and a pistol or two with a durk and knife on his belt.

The anonymous author does not give any explanation of what "claymore" means, giving us the impression that his audience would have understood it. It must have already been in circulation in English, even though it doesn't seem to survive in other texts from this time period.

"Claymore" appears several times in accounts about the 1745 Jacobite Rising, such as the materials collected by the Reverend Robert Forbes between 1746 and 1775 and published much later (1895-96) as the three-volume *The Lyon in Mourning*. According to some former soldiers, recalling earlier events, "claymore" was the war-cry of the Jacobite army.

"Claymore" began to circulate more widely after appearing in travelogues of the 1770s, written by the antiquarians and well-heeled tourists who came to visit the Scottish Highlands. Thomas Pennant recorded it in 1772 as "cly-more," while both Samuel Johnson and James Boswell, who travelled Scotland together in 1773, give it as "glaymore." The term was further employed by Lowland writers such as Robert Burns and Walter Scott at the turn of the nineteenth century, who brought it to new audiences in songs and novels.

In 1803, for example, Lowland Scottish poet Thomas Campbell (1777-1844) published a poem entitled "Lochiel's Warning" about the Battle of Culloden which portrays the Jacobite army as consisting of claymore-wielding Highland clans:

But woe to his kindred, and woe to his cause,

When Albin her claymore indignantly draws;
When her bonneted chieftains to victory crowd,
Clanranald the dauntless, and Moray the proud,
All plaided and plumed in their tartan array ...

"Claymore" is a borrowing of the Gaelic term *claidheamh mór*, which simply means "big sword." In reality, different kinds of swords were used in the Highlands at different times. The two-handed sword popularized by Hollywood was used from the fifteenth through the seventeenth century. Images of this weapon can be found on the sculptured gravestones of many of the powerful leaders of the Gaelic world of that time period, symbolizing their military power. It was referred to at the time in English simply as "the two-handed sword."

The two-handed sword retained an iconic status among the Highland élite into the seventeenth century, although by then it was being replaced by the basket-hilted broadsword. These newcomers were initially imported from Germany and Spain, but smiths in the Scottish Lowlands were soon forging their own imitations.

Regardless, they were often referred to in Gaelic as *lannan Spàinnteach* "Spanish blades" or even just *Spàinnteach* "Spaniard" alone. In a poem to one of the MacLean chieftains of Duart named Lachlann, probably composed in the mid-seventeenth century, the subject is described with his weaponry:

Spàinnteach làidir fulangach
An làimh a' churaidh chliùitich,
'S an sgiath bu tric an taisbeanadh
Air ghaoirdein deas nan lùth-chleas.

A strong, sturdy Spaniard
In the hand of the famous warrior
With the targe that was frequently shown
On the fine, athletic arm.

There was another more descriptive term for the basket-hilted broadsword in Gaelic, however: *claidheamh cùil a' chinn aisnich*, which could be translated as "sword of the ribbed handle." The elegy composed for the renowned pan-Gaelic warrior Alasdair mac Colla, who died fighting in Ireland in 1647, depicts him as wielding a blade of this description, which has been preserved at Loughan Castle.

The Gaelic term *claidheamh mór* may not have come into common currency until the eighteenth century. The first surviving use of *claidheamh mór* comes from the Jacobite poet Alasdair mac Mhaighstir Alasdair. In a song rallying Highlanders to join the Prince's cause in 1745, he urges them:

No na mealadh mi mo ghòirseid,
An daga, 'bhiodag, 's an claidheamh mór-sa,
Mur h-eil mi toileach a dhol leo chomhrag
A dh'fhuadach Uilleim gu Hanòbhar.

May I never enjoy my gorget,
Pistol, dirk or claymore
Unless I am willing to go into battle with them
To expel William to Hanover.

The image of the sword-bearing Celtic warrior has left a mark on literature and history that goes back to Roman times. One of the words for sword in Latin, *gladius*, which is the root of the well-known word "gladiator," was borrowed from the Celtic rivals of the Romans.

King Arthur's sword Excalibur is one of the most celebrated swords in European literature and it too is derived from earlier Celtic prototypes. The early medieval Irish tale *Táin Bó Cuailgne* names the Ulster hero Fergus mac Róich as the owner of a sword named *Caladbolg* or *Caladcholg* (depending on the version of the tale). In the medieval Welsh tale *Culhwch ac Olwen*, King Arthur was said to be the owner of a sword named *Caledfwlch*. These two names are closely related, but whether the Welsh borrowed the Gaelic term or vice-versa is not clear. When Geoffrey of Monmouth retold the Arthurian legend in his Latin volume on the kings of Britain, he adapted the name of the sword as *Caliburnus*, which was further transformed in the French romances about Arthur as Excalibur.

The magical swords of Celtic literatures have continued to exert an influence on their cousins in modern science fiction and fantasy, at least to some degree. The magical sword of the Gaelic folk tales of both Ireland and the Scottish Highlands was called *Claidheamh-Solais*, which could be translated literally as "light saber." Although Gaelic tradition is not the only one that conjures bright, shining weapons, it is not difficult to see a distant echo of Highland folk tales in the Star Wars universe.

Blackmail

The word "blackmail" is used in English nowadays to describe a form of extortion where an unscrupulous person exploits incriminating evidence about another person in order to coerce them to do something. Blackmail typically requires paying an exorbitant sum of money to prevent compromising details of a person's life from being revealed to others, although other forms of manipulation, such as "emotional blackmail" and "cyber blackmail," are also known.

The earliest surviving occurrences of the word "blackmail" in English were recorded in legal records of the sixteenth-century Scottish Lowlands, such as a passage from a Scottish Act of 1567 describing it as a kind of rural protection racket: "Diverse subjects of the inland, take and sit under their assurance, paying them blackmail, and permitting them to reive, harry, and oppress their neighbors."

"Blackmail" appears in English legal contexts in the eighteenth century but it is likely Walter Scott's celebrated 1814 novel *Waverly*, depicting the Highlands during the 1745 Jacobite Rising, that brought the word popular attention. In the tale, a young Scottish gentlewoman explains the meaning of the word to the English visitor:

> "A sort of protection-money that Low-Country gentlemen and heritors, lying near the Highlands, pay to some Highland chief, that he may neither

do them harm himself, nor suffer it to be done to them by others; and then if your cattle are stolen, you have only to send him word, and he will recover them; or it may be, he will drive away cows from some distant place, where he has a quarrel, and give them to you to make up your loss."

Scottish Highlanders are commonly depicted as thieves and criminals in anglophone sources, as though they rejected basic principles of law, private property, and civilized moral codes. The Gaelic perspective on these matters is quite different. For one, cattle raiding was a well-recognized and legitimate form of aggression between clans, one that had its own set of protocols and cultural norms. Raiding was a coming of age ritual for the aspiring heirs of chieftains who were expected to be able to lead a foray against their enemies, such as Martin Martin describes in the late 1600s about practices that had already become rare by that time:

> It was usual for the Captain to lead them, to make a desperate Incursion upon some Neighbour or other that they were in Feud with; and they were oblig'd to bring by open force the Cattel they found in the Lands they attack'd, or to die in the Attempt.

> After the Performance of this Atchievement, the young Chieftain was ever after reputed valiant and worthy of Government, and such as were of his Retinue acquir'd the like Reputation. This Custom being reciprocally us'd among them, was not reputed Robbery, for the Damage which one Tribe sustain'd by this Essay of the Chieftain of another, was repair'd when their Chieftain came in his turn to make his Specimin ...

On the other hand, political and economic disruptions in seventeenth-century Scotland had very destabilizing effects on the Highlands, as clans clashed in new or intensified struggles, dispossessed clansmen resorted to desperate measures for survival, and the central government had little interest in finding ways to resolve these issues. Blackmail can be understood as a means by which Highlanders sought to minimize disorderly and errant behavior within their own locales. An account recorded in Gaelic in the mid-1800s from Loch Lomond-side provides a valuable inside perspective indicating that the practices had been implemented in that region in a very formal and legalistic manner:

> There was a contract between the laird of Arrochar and the other lairds with the farmers on the lands of Lennox that they were to pay to the former (the laird of Arrochar) blackmail for every head of cattle in their possession;

and that the laird of Arrochar was to protect them in return from the inroads of thieves and robbers. Should any of the cattle of those who paid blackmail be either carried off as spoil or stolen, the laird of Arrochar was bound to find the same and restore them to the owners; and if he could not find them, he was bound to provide equally good cattle for them, or else pay for them in money. In consequence of this, the laird of Arrochar kept a host between the north end of Loch Long and Loch Lomond, and gave each man of them a piece of land ...

"Blackmail" corresponds directly to the Gaelic term *màl dubh*. *Màl* was borrowed from Anglo-Saxon at an early period, as it appears in medieval Gaelic texts referring to money paid as a form of tribute. It is now the normal Gaelic word meaning "rent." The color element *dubh* "black" may refer to the fact that the payment was itself made in cattle, and until the late nineteenth century, the vast majority of Highland cattle were black. Alternatively, it may simply indicate the negative connotations of the burden of payment.

Spree

People may speak excitedly of going on a shopping spree, or of the disagreeable after-effects of having gone on a drunken spree. There are also crime sprees and even spree killing. The dictionary definition of "spree" is a bout of unrestrained or rowdy behavior, often accompanied by drinking. This word entered anglophone speech at the beginning of the nineteenth century, apparently with strong Scottish associations.

William Lillie, a plowman living near Buchan in the north-east of Scotland, penned a satirical poem in 1812 about Napoleon's expedition to Russia that conveys the usage of the term and confirms the pronunciation through the word with which it rhymes: "Twa Emperors ance had a bit o' a spree ... I believe they fell out 'cause they cud na agree."

The quest for the origins of the word "spree" is complicated by the fact that the word "spray" was also used in early nineteenth-century Scotland with the more specific meaning of a flurry of drinking. An early occurrence appears in Walter Scott's 1819 *Legend of Montrose*, where he portrays a soldier given to binging at the public house:

> Further, it must not be denied, that when the day of receiving his dividends came round, the Sergeant was apt to tarry longer at the Wallace Arms of an evening, than was consistent with strict temperance, or indeed with his worldly interest; for upon these occasions, his compotators sometimes contrived to flatter his partialities by singing Jacobite songs, and drinking confusion to Bonaparte, and the health of the Duke of Wellington, until the Sergeant was not only flattered into paying the whole reckoning, but occasionally induced to lend small sums to his interested companions. After such sprays, as he called them, were over, and his temper once more cool, he seldom failed to thank God ...

Spray and spree, then, are closely related words found in vernacular usage in the Scottish Lowlands by the beginning of the nineteenth century, with no obvious origins in English or other Germanic languages. They are most likely borrowings from Scottish Gaelic, but there are two different Gaelic words with similar pronunciation that likely explain the pedigree of spree and spray.

The first of these is *spréidh*, a Gaelic word in use by the eleventh century primarily meaning "cattle, livestock." As the Gaelic economy was a pastoral one centered on cattle, *spréidh* acquired the secondary meaning of "wealth, property." Not only did aggression between rival clans often get acted out in the form of cattle raids, but Gaels considered Lowlanders as unwelcome interlopers on territory that had rightfully belonged to the Gaels themselves, and therefore as legitimate targets of cattle raids as a matter of principle. One of the most explicit statements of this nature is in a love song attributed to Rachel MacGregor of Rannoch, probably composed in the seventeenth century:

Cuime am biomaid gun eudail
Agus spréidh aig na Gallaibh?

Why should we want for riches
When the Lowlanders have cattle?

The Gaelic word *spréidh* was borrowed into Lowland Scots by the fifteenth century, taking a range of forms such as "spreth," "spreitht," "spraich," "spraigh," and "sprauch," and acquiring the meaning "plunder, booty, stolen animals." It was also used in seventeenth-century Lowland Scots to refer to the act of plundering or raiding. It is fairly easy to see how its use could be extended to refer to any merry, roguish or mischievous outing, and its fricative ending curtailed. The comments of traveller Thomas Pennant, during his 1769 tour in the Highlands, reflect the sense of an exciting adventure:

> Highlanders at that time esteemed the open theft of cattle, or the making a spreith (as they called it) by no means dishonorable; and the young men considered it as a piece of gallantry, by which they recommend themselves to their mistresses.

The other Scottish Gaelic word that seems to have contributed to this verbal cocktail is *spreadh* "burst, explode, crackle." It can be traced to the early medieval period in the form *spréd*, a noun signifying a spark or, metaphorically, vigor or affection. This evolved during the later medieval period into the form *spréidid* or *spréigid*, a verb meaning "to scatter, disperse." The Irish scholar Thomas O'Rahilly recognized in the early twentieth century that this word, in its Scottish Gaelic incarnation, was the likely source for English "spree," noting that the parallel usage in English of the word "burst" for a bout of drunkenness.

These two Gaelic words, then, conveying the sense of a burst of energy causing people to go into motion for the purposes of an exciting outing, sometimes stimulated by the consumption of alcohol, found their way into the English "spree." Don't blame Highlanders, however, if you can't restrain yourself at the shops or the pub.

Cateran

You can get a sense of rural Scotland as it was in the pre-modern era by following the Cateran Trail, a 103-kilometer circular walking route that criss-crosses the boundaries between Highlands and Lowlands. This commemorative pathway invokes the caterans, who are first mentioned by this name in Lowland Scots in the legislation of King Robert II in the late fourteenth century, complaining that they were "takand their gudis be force and violence" (taking their goods by force and violence).

This was the earliest of many Lowland condemnations of bands roving the Highlands and venturing further afield to commit crimes of theft and brutality. Lowlanders generalized the misdeeds of the caterans as being essentially Highland vices, so that Lowland stereotypes of Gaels are based to a large degree on the transgressions of outlaws who turned to banditry and bloodshed out of desperation.

William Dunbar composed a Lowland Scots poem in the early sixteenth century which praises a member of the king's court – probably in a satirical manner – for, among other things, his heavy-handed treatment of unruly subjects in the Highlands:

Full mony catherein hes he chaist
And cummerid mony Helland gaist
Among thay dully glennis ...

(Full many caterans has he chased
And pursued many Highland ghosts
Among the gloomy glens ...)

Although the caterans were invoked from time to time in Lowland texts, it was the literature of Walter Scott that made the word familiar to a wider anglophone audience, starting with his 1814 blockbuster *Waverly*. The protagonist in the story, Edward Waverly, an English gentleman, is visiting a friend of his uncle's at an estate near the Highlands when an unexpected crisis arises:

'Your breakfast will be a disturbed one, Captain Waverley. A party of Caterans have come down upon us last night, and have driven off all our milch cows.'

'A party of Caterans?'

'Yes; robbers from the neighbouring Highlands. We used to be quite free from them while we paid blackmail to Fergus Mac-Ivor Vich Ian Vohr; but my father thought it unworthy of his rank and birth to pay it any longer, and so this disaster has happened.'

It is this encounter which draws Waverly into the Gaelic world and the Jacobite movement, and the reader along with him.

The Lowland Scots word "cateran" is derived from the Gaelic noun *ceatharn*, "a war band." When they operated as gangs they made themselves very unpopular in the Gaelic world itself: *Cormac's Glossary* claimed that the word was made of elements meaning "battle" and "slaughter." In the sixteenth century it was explained in another Gaelic text as being derived from *cioth Ifrinn* "a shower of Hell."

This word was typically rendered in English as "kerne" in Irish contexts, and it occasionally appears in this form in Scottish sources as well, such as in the clan history of the Campbells of Craignish: "... younger Brothers tho' even of great Families having in those days no other patrimonie assigned them than their Sword and a Band of Kearne who commonly ravaged out a patrimony for them wherever they could compass it ..."

Caterans and the mayhem they created did not reflect the ideals of Highland clan society but were rather a symptom of socio-economic deficits that were exacerbated during the crises of the seventeenth century:

> As masterless or 'broken men', the caterans had all but thrown over the social constraints of clanship. As racketeers, they specialised in extorting blackmail from Lowland farmers as an insurance against their removal of livestock. As enforcers, they hired themselves out primarily to Lowland landlords wishing to resolve territorial disputes by intimidation. These bands periodically became more numerous as a result of the social dislocation in the aftermath of the civil wars of the 1640s, of the severely prolonged famine of the 1690s and of the political purging verging on 'ethnic cleansing' in the aftermath of the 'Forty-Five rebellion.

The word *ceatharn* in Gaelic itself did not necessarily refer to ruffians who had been dispossessed of land and clan membership. In fact, a mid-eighteenth-century Highland antiquarian uses this name for the handpicked retinue kept by Highland chieftains:

> Leaping was another exercise in great esteem among the Scots of former days. Every chief, who had spirit enough to support the dignity of his name

and fortune, kept a band of youth and active warriors continually about his person, one of whose qualifications it was necessary should be agility in this kind of exercise. These warriors, or *Ceatharn*, were constantly employed in manly exercises and recreations in time of peace, and served the chief as a kind of body guards.

A single member of a *ceatharn* "war-band" is called a *ceatharnach* (pl. *ceatharnaich*) in Gaelic. It was used of trained military men in earlier eras, but by the nineteenth century could simply mean "hero; stout, trusty peasant; strong robust man." In a depiction of a shinty game written in 1848, for example, the players are described as *ceatharnaich*.

It is important to highlight the fact that not only did Lowland Scots "cateran" and Gaelic *ceatharn* have different connotations and associations, but that the Gaelic noun has been constantly evolving to take on different meanings and usages.

The Cateran Society was founded in 1998 to revive the martial arts of the Scottish Highlands, particularly Highland broadsword fencing. Nine historical manuals, written in the eighteenth and nineteenth centuries, were used as the basis of a curriculum divided into five levels. The Cateran Society now has branches all over the world, with a particularly active franchise in Siberia. Who would have guessed that the Cateran Trail could be extended so far?

Galloglass

The word "galloglass" began to appear in English in the early sixteenth century, during the reign of King Henry VIII, in documents about the conflict in Ireland between English colonial forces and native Gaelic lords. Irish military strength drew greatly upon heavily-armed mercenaries recruited from the north-west of Scotland called in English the "galloglass" (sometimes spelled in other ways like "gallowglass"). These troops were usually placed in the rear-guard of fighting units to protect the Irish warriors from pursuers as they retreated.

Although Gaelic texts began to refer to them as a distinct group in 1290, they must have been active in Ireland for at least a century beforehand. Mercenary forces began to settle on the lands of the native Irish lords they served in the fourteenth century, and these reciprocal relationships reforged social bonds across the Gaelic worlds of Ireland and Scotland into the seventeenth century.

The play *Macbeth* mentions this warrior class by name and portrays the political dominance of Clan Donald across the Irish Sea, even if Shakespeare was incorrect to assume that the galloglasses were active during the reign of this Scottish king (the eleventh century):

The merciless Macdonwald,
Worthy to be a rebel, for to that
The multiplying villainies of nature
Do swarm upon him, from the Western Isles
Of kerns and gallowglasses is supplied ...

As we might expect, Walter Scott also makes mention of the Gaelic mercenaries in his ballad *The Lord of the Isles*, published in 1815, depicting the return of King Robert Bruce of Scotland from exile in Ireland. *Gallowglass* was also the title of a BBC miniseries broadcast in 1993, based on a novel by Barbara Vine (Ruth Rendell) published in 1990.

"Galloglass" is an anglicization of the Gaelic term *gall-óglaigh* (sing. *gall-óglach*). This term meant literally "foreign young-warrior" although *gall* was used in the thirteenth century specifically for people who were, at least in part, of Norse descent but had become largely Gaelicized. These mercenaries were drawn mostly from the Hebrides and western seaboard of Scotland.

While the military might and prowess of these warriors is amply attested in Gaelic tradition, their reliance on the healing skills of their wives and female relations is more subtly encoded in Gaelic plant terminology: lemon balm is called *lus mná an Ghall-óglaigh* "the herb of the Galloglass's wife" in early modern texts. Lemon balm can be used for a wide variety of healing purposes, from pain relief to reducing stress and boosting cognitive functions. The galloglasses may have been successful due to the medicinal practices of their womenfolk as much as the deadly blows of their weapons!

Sport and Music

Strathspey

Over the last two and a half centuries the strathspey - actually short for "strathspey reel" - has become the most characteristically Scottish form of instrumental music. Classical composers such as Beethoven, Schubert, and Chopin were inspired by this distinctive genre, especially its "Scotch snaps." Many of the dances in Highland Dancing, Scottish Country Dancing, and Cape Breton step-dances are choreographed specifically for tunes of the strathspey genre, whether played on fiddle or bagpipe.

Srath Spé is the Gaelic name for the area called "Speyside" or "the Spey Valley" in English. Although it is best known today as a major hub of whisky production, it is also likely to be the birthplace of the unique style of dance music that bears its name. The Menzies manuscript of 1749 provides the earliest examples of tunes explicitly called "strathspey." Reverend Dr. William Thomson, a minister from the Scottish Lowlands who also played the fiddle, toured the Highlands in 1785. His travelogue, published under the pseudonym Thomas Newte in 1791, offers an origin legend:

> Strathspey is celebrated for its reels, a species of music that happily unites gaiety with grace, moving now with measured step and flow, and now at a quick and sudden pace. ... With regard to the first composers, or even performers of strathspey reels, there are not any certain accounts. According to the tradition of the country, the first who played them were the Browns of Kincardin, to whom are ascribed a few of the most ancient tunes. After these men, the Cummings of Freuchie, now Castle-Grant, were in the highest estimation for their knowledge and execution in strathspey music; and most of the tunes handed down to us are certainly of their composing. A successive race of musicians, like people of the same caste in Hindustan, succeeded each other for many generations. The last of that name, famous for his skill in music, was John Roy Cumming. He died about thirty years ago and there are many persons, still alive, who speak of his performance with the greatest rapture ... Before I quit my present subject, I shall just take notice, that the Strathspey is to the common Scotch Reel what a Spanish Fandango is to a French Cotillon.

While the development of the strathspey must have been more complicated than this brief sketch, it nonetheless contains some useful tidbits of information. The Baroque violin arrived in Scotland in the second half of the seventeenth century, and we can expect that it was accompanied by a repertoire of tunes suited for it, including social dance tunes. Dance was considered by Europeans of that era to be an essential aspect of deportment, manners, and training for the youth, as well as entertainment for all. These forms of social dance spread quickly, especially because they were tied to aspirations of upward economic mobility that had been newly enabled through education and social refinement.

The native aristocracy of the Highlands provided the patronage necessary to support the training and maintenance of professional musicians. The Spey Valley is not far from the Scottish Lowlands and the Highland families who lived there, who also acted as patrons for local musicians, were interested in European music and culture. They also had social ties that crossed the Highland-Lowland divide, and indeed, even extended into continental Europe.

The Grants are likely one of the pivotal families in this history of musical evolution. They had been the patrons of the Cummings of Freuchie, who had started as bagpipers, since at least the seventeenth century. The Cummings seem to have begun acquiring skills on the fiddle in the late seventeenth century. Over time, Highland musicians such as the Cummings would have adapted mainstream European social dance music to match the styles and idioms natural to a Gaelic ear.

The most distinctive feature of the strathspey reel – the dotted rhythms of the so-called "Scotch Snap" – seems to reflect the characteristics of Gaelic speech and song, in which vowel length is significant and most words receive a heavy initial stress. A recent examination of rhythmic patterns in folk songs has found the snap to be twice as common in Scottish Gaelic songs than in Lowland Scots songs and almost four times more common in Scottish Gaelic songs than in English songs.

Memoirs about the 1745 Jacobite Rising contain scenes which include dancing to "Strathspey-inflected" dance music. When Prince Charles visited Lude House near Blair Atholl, in the central Highlands, for example, "he was very chearful and took his share in several dances, such as minuets, Highland reels (the first reel the Prince called for was, 'This is not mine ain house,' etc.), and a Strathspey minuet."

When he was in hiding as a fugitive in the Highlands, the Prince encountered young women at a shieling and attempted to get them to dance with him. He is reported to have said: "Come, my lasses, what would you think to dance a Highland reel with me? We cannot have a bag-pipe just now, but I shall sing you a Strathspey reel." It is from this same decade that we have the first surviving transcriptions of fiddle tunes composed in Scotland that feature Scotch snaps and have "strathspey" in their titles.

Simon Fraser was a native of the Central Highlands and an accomplished fiddle player. His 1816 collection *The Airs and Melodies peculiar to the Highlands of Scotland and the Isles* contains a tune dedicated to the locality with the bi-lingual title "*Srath-Spè*, 'Strathspey.' The Native Country of the Sprightly Dance," which he notes should be played in "Slow Strathspey Style." The endnote about this tune states:

> In passing through the district of Strathspey, the traveller may be apt to forget, that among the long ranges of firwood and heath on each side, originated that sprightly style of performing and dancing the music which bears its name, now in universal request from the Spey to the Ganges. If the poets now take up the subject of some of the airs produced on its banks, it

may become as renowned as a classic stream, as it is famous for giving birth to so much of our national and captivating amusement.

Virtuoso fiddlers such as James Scott Skinner did indeed continue to champion the strathspey in the nineteenth century, to the extent that it has become quintessentially Scottish in the eyes of many.

The Strathspey is to Scotland what the jig is to Ireland, the contra dance or the hornpipe to England, the Czardas to Hungary, the Tarantella to Italy, or the Cachucha to Spain - it enshrines the gayest spirit and life of the nation.

Croon

The word "croon" in modern English usually describes singing in a soft, low, or emotional manner. The invention of electric microphones in the early twentieth century enabled such soft and subtle tones to be detected and broadcast to large audiences, giving rise to the nickname "The Crooners" to singers from the 1920s and 1930s such as Gene Austin, Bing Crosby, and Frank Sinatra.

The word "croon" is well attested from the eighteenth century onwards to describe lamentation, singing in a low register, the bellowing of cattle, and the purring of cats. One of the earliest and most evocative uses comes from the first Scottish opera, *The Gentle Shepherd*, whose lyrics were written by Lowland poet Alan Ramsay in 1725.

> Here Mausy lives, a witch that for sma' price,
> Can cast her cantrips, an gie me advice:
> She can owercast the nicht, an cloud the muin,
> An mak the deils obedient to her cruin.

The rhyme between "muin" (modern "moon") and "cruin" (modern "croon") confirms the pronunciation. Until the term was popularized across English dialects by the Lowland poet Robert Burns in the late eighteenth century, "croon" was restricted to northern English and Scottish vernacular usage.

The standard etymology of the word traces it via Middle English *croyne* back to Middle Dutch *cronen* "to groan or moan." Even if we accept this as the main lineage of Scots "croon," it was likely also affected by the term *crònan* in Scottish Gaelic.

This word appears in a Gaelic poem composed in the tenth century describing the sound of bees as *crónán séim* "soft crooning." It is used in a number of other early Gaelic texts to mean "humming, purring, droning, low-range singing." An early legal tract states that a cat that is able to croon and guard barn, mill, and kiln against mice is worth three cows.

While it has been suggested that the Gaelic *crònan* may have also been borrowed from a Germanic language at a very early period, it quickly made its way into core vocabulary for discussing music, song, and orality.

Crònan can be found in Gaelic texts written in Scotland from the late fifteenth century onwards. The deer hind is described as *crònanach* "murmuring" in the idyllic and nostalgic song "Òran na Comhachaig," dated to the late sixteenth century. Gaelic poet Iain Lom MacDonald praised the warrior Alasdair mac Colla after the Battle of Auldearn in 1645 returning victorious,

> *Le saighdearan laghach*
> *An àm gabhail an rathaid*
> *Leis am bu mhiannach bhith gabhail a' chrònain.*

> With his fine soldiers

Who at the outset of their march
Loved to sing his croon.

The best known use of the term in Gaelic literary history relates to another of the accomplished poets of the seventeenth century, Màiri nighean Alasdair Ruaidh, also known in English as "Mary MacLeod." According to oral traditions recorded in the nineteenth century, Màiri had been banished to Mull by a MacLeod chieftain because of worries that her excessive praise of his children had brought them bad luck and even illness. The chieftain allowed to her return to his court on the condition that she not compose any more tributes to them. Soon after coming back, one of the chieftain's sons recovered from an illness and Màiri composed a song to him in celebration. Upon being confronted about this, Màiri answered, "It's not a song, it's only a *crònan*."

This dismissal of crooning, in contrast to the more formal and polished songs of the entrenched establishment of professional male poets, is not unlike the hostile press that "The Crooners" received in the 1930s. It is usually futile, however, to try to stop people from expressing themselves in ways that bring them meaning and pleasure. As the traditional Gaelic proverb says, *Is ann air a shon fhéin a nì an cat an crònan* "It is for itself that the cat croons."

Boogie

The slang term "boogie" has several related usages in colloquial American English: to dance energetically, a style of Blues music, a house party featuring music and dance, to leave quickly, and to have sex. It is difficult to be certain of its relationship with many other words that sound similar, not least because similar words occur across numerous languages. Anatoly Liberman explored these complexities in a blog post in the *The Oxford Etymologist* series:

> Imitative words are similar all over the world, don't obey so-called phonetic laws, and are easily borrowed. ... *Boogie*, as in *boogie-woogie*, is believed to be a West African coinage, and, if it is true that boogie originally meant "prostitute," we are dealing with a social bugaboo. Speakers all over the world use the sound complex *boog-* ~ *bog-* for naming similar objects. Bogey emerged as a member of a large family. Old Bogey is the Devil, a bug, a bugbear. *Bogus*, initially, as it seems, part of counterfeiters' slang, is, like most words being discussed here, of unknown etymology. It may well be a relative of bogey.

Given the vast range of ethnic groups and linguistic communities that contributed to the underworld slang of American English, it is futile to hope for a singular and definitive origin for the word "boogie." It does seem worthwhile to suggest, however, that Scottish Gaelic word *bogadh* made a contribution to this energetic and erotic cocktail.

In Scottish Gaelic, the verb *bog* (verbal noun *bogadh*) has several meanings: "dip, immerse, steep; soften, moisten; move, bob, wag; float." A dog wagging his tail is *a' bogadh earbaill*. It is used in a Gaelic song-poem composed about the year 1732 in a context associated with music, dance, and sexual excitement:

> *Crith-chiùil air m' ugan g'a bogadh*
> *'S mo chompar uile làn beadraidh;*
> *Tein' éibhinn am uchd air fadadh*
> *'S mi air fad air dannsa leigeil.*

> A musical quaver causing my throat to shake
> And my whole body is full of flirting
> In my breast a bonfire is kindled
> And I'm completely possessed by dancing.

Our knowledge of slang words and idioms for sexual activity in Scottish Gaelic over the last several centuries is fairly limited, largely due to the efforts of church ministers in the nineteenth and early twentieth centuries to limit their use in print, as well as other literary gatekeepers who followed their lead. *Bogadh* is one of the words used in Gaelic poems composed in the eighteenth century to refer to sexual intercourse. When it is declined in the genitive case, *bogadh* becomes *bogaidh*, pronounced almost identically to "boogie" in modern English.

One of the songs in which *bogadh* appears (in its variant form *boga*) is a celebration of the carnal lifestyle of the libertine, composed by George MacKenzie (c.1655 – c.1735) of Gruinard, Wester Ross.

Nach éibhinn am boga nodha,
Their gach té ri chéile
"B'e m' eudail a bheireadh dhomh e!"

What fun is the boogie noogie,
The girls all say to each other,
"It's my darling who would give it to me!"

Highland poetess Sìleas na Ceapaich (c.1660 – c.1729) composed a song-poem in response to MacKenzie's ribaldry to warn her daughters of the likely costs of yielding themselves to flattering young men and of the rejection they might have to endure. This poem also has several instances of the term *boga(dh)*, as in this quatrain:

Gheibh sibh gealladh pòsaidh
Nuair a thòisicheas boga-bhriseadh,
'S nuair a gheibh e 'n ruaig ud:
"Beir uam i! Chan fhaca mis' i!"

You'll get a promise of marriage
When you lose your virginity
And when he's had his conquest:
"Take her away! I've never seen her!"

Although boogie fever may have spread to America from several origins, Scottish Highlanders should not be afraid to claim some stake in it, despite the disapproval of puritanical ministers and concerned parents.

Fore

A shout of "fore!" on the golf course warns bystanders to beware of balls flying through the air. The earliest surviving record of the term is in a manual written for golfers in 1857 but it indicates that the signal was already in widespread use. Attempts to explain the origins of the exclamation usually claim that it is a shortening of the word "before" or that it refers to the area in front of the golfer in various ways.

It is surprising for a game that has such strong a historical association with Scotland that so few people have attempted to explore the possibility of a Gaelic origin for the word. The noun *faire* means "watching, guarding, outlook" and is a by-form of *aire* meaning "attention, perception, heed." A *fear-faire* is a watchman and *facal-faire* is a watchword. *Faire* was used in both medieval Gaelic Scotland and Ireland as an exclamation meaning, "Look!" as well as "Take care! Beware!" The seventeenth-century Irish scholar Geoffrey Keating observed that anglophones were aware of the Gaelic exclamation.

In a song composed by Rob Dunn of Sutherland after the Act of Proscription in 1746 prohibited civilian men in the Highlands from wearing tartans or plaids and from possessing weapons, the poet warns the king not to impose overly harsh measures that would not differentiate between friend and foe, saying, *Faire, faire, Rìgh Deòrsa!* "Beware, beware, King George!" One of the early novels in Gaelic, published in 1913, portrays the Highlands leading up to the 1745 Jacobite Rising. In one scene, a character has an argument with MacLeod of Dunvegan and attempts to make him listen, saying *Faire! Faire! Fhir Dhùn Bheagain!*

There are two traditional Gaelic exclamations in which this word appears: *faire-faire!* is an expression of surprise or dismay, as if to imply "Now look at what's happened!" It appears in a poem composed in the early eighteenth century about the MacKenzies. The interjection *fire-faire* is used to express exasperation, frustration, or concern. It can be found in a bagpipe song about Cameron of Lochiall, likely from the seventeenth century, as well as in a lullaby of a similar age for the MacLeods of Dunvegan, protecting the infant heir from the malevolence of fairies. Both of these expressions are used in a song by

Ruaidhri MacMhuirich (*An Clàrsair Dall*) composed shortly after the death of his patron, Iain Breac MacLeod of Dunvegan, in 1693.

The exclamation *fire-faire* has an exact parallel in the Lowland Scots interjection "firy fary" or "furye farye" with the same meaning. It was first recorded in the poetry of Alexander Montgomerie, a native of Ayrshire who lived in the second half of the sixteenth century. Some thirteen Gaelic words or phrases appear in the work of Montgomerie, who probably spoke Gaelic. This expression can be found in at least one other Lowland text before the end of the seventeenth century. The similarity between these two exclamations is too close to be coincidental: either the Lowland Scots borrowed from the Highlanders, or the other way around.

The word "fary" in Lowland Scots has several meanings, from supernatural beings, and the Otherworld realm that they inhabit, to illusion or a confused or agitated state of mind. The word "fary" appears in the work of Robert Henryson (c.1460 - 1500), William Dunbar (c.1460 - c.1530) and Gavin Douglas (c.1474 - 1522) with these latter senses, conveying distress, perturbation, and delirium. Despite mutual distrust and hostility between Highlands and Lowlands, many Gaelic words appear in the poetry of Lowland poets of this era, particularly in the work of Dunbar. It's not difficult to see how these Lowland usages arose from the Gaelic *faire* if we think about the circumstances in which the alarm was sounded: one of danger, anxiety, and commotion, especially during military conflict.

The heightened sense of awareness during battle seems to induce an altered state of consciousness that the Gaels associated with the supernatural. From early medieval sources, we know that gods and goddesses associated with death and panic appeared on the battlefield along with the heroes, to encourage or taunt them, or even fight the warriors themselves. Tales of these Otherworld encounters continued into the early modern period. Take, for example, Gerald of Wales' description of a paranormal event during the Anglo-Norman's invasion of Ireland:

> Suddenly there were, it seemed, countless thousands of troops rushing upon them from all sides and engulfing all before them in the ferocity of their attack. This was accompanied by no small din of arms and clashing of axes, and a fearsome shouting which filled the heavens. Apparitions of this sort used to occur frequently in Ireland around military expeditions.

It is precisely this complex of ideas - agitation, excitement, derangement, and the Otherworld - that appears in the Lowland Scots term "fary" and has also fed into the modern English word "fairy."

Only highly competitive golfers might become as aggressive as warriors on a field of combat, but high-velocity golf balls can cause serious injury. You can help others pay attention so that they don't get knocked on the head and suffer bouts of delirium and hallucination: shout *faire!* Or "fore!"

Shindig

A shindig, in American slang, is a frolicsome party featuring music and dance. This word is enshrined in a popular annual dance event, Shindig on the Green, held in Asheville, North Carolina, since 1967 celebrating Southern Appalachian folk culture. *The Shindig* was also the title of a short animated film starring Mickey Mouse released in 1930 which depicts the character and his friends enjoying a barn dance.

The noun "shindig" began to appear in written sources in the 1840s about rural settlements in the United States. In 1848, for example, Charles A. Hentz remarked that he encountered a fiddle and a Virginia reel at a "genuine piney-woods shindig" in Port Jackson, Florida. In 1864, it was noted that an effective way to find recruits for black regiments would be to visit shindigs, which were popular among enslaved African-Americans.

From the get-go, English-speakers tried to explain the odd term by interpreting it as an activity that could involve blows to the legs. In his travelogue *Sights in the gold region*, about a journey to California during the 1849 Gold Rush, Theodore Johnson of New Jersey wrote, "One of our party commenced a regular hoe-down, knocking his shins with heavy boots." John Bartlett's 1859 *Dictionary of Americanisms* contains the entry "Shin-Dig" with the definition "a blow on the shins." These seem to be fanciful folk-etymologies, however, rather than accurate accounts of the historical origin of the word, especially as there are no known folk dances from rural America that have such movements.

Unravelling the history of the word "shindig" requires examining a couple of other words with similar sounds and associations. The first of these is the noun "shindy," which begins to appear in the 1820s with the senses of "a party; a brawl, uproar, riot." The origins of the word "shindy" are still uncertain but have been noted to be likely related to the word "shinty."

Shinty is a ferocious stick-and-ball game once played all over northern Britain but now surviving primarily in the Scottish Highlands. The game has gone by a variety of names, including "schynnie," "shinney," and "chinnup." While "shinney" can be found by the year 1600, "shinty" seems to have become the dominant form in Lowland Scotland after about 1700. There is nearly a millennium and half of references to the game in the Gaelic literature of both Ireland and Scotland. It is generally called *iomain* "driving" or *camanachd* "use of bent stick" in modern Scottish Gaelic.

Shinty was a highly popular game in rural Scotland in the past and allowed rivalries to be hashed out during the seasonal festivities of the New Year, Christmas, or Halloween, depending on local tradition and conditions. The game highlights the energy and dexterity of the players, and it was customary in some Highland parishes to hold a dance afterward for the entertainment and pleasure of all. A correspondent to a Highland newspaper in 1870 testified to the crowds and commotion that could attend these New Year games:

Every able-bodied male inhabitant, from both sides of the country, for a distance of many miles each way, meet on a common near the centre of the parish, where a great match of playing the club is held between the two sides of the district. ... I have seen as many as 2,000 men engaged in these contests, besides a vast number of visitors. Usually the stakes were simply the honour of either half of the district, but occasionally a hogs-head of whiskey was given to the winners by the proprietor. This liberality led to such scenes of drinking, and sometimes of fighting, that in recent years he wisely refrained from a present in the train of which were consequences so disagreeable.

As in the case of the shindig, some observers tried explain the origin of the word "shinty" as having something to do with bruised or broken shins, but this too is imaginative speculation rather than informed analysis. The name for the game in anglophone Scotland - moving away from "shinny" and toward "shinty" - seems to have been influenced by the Gaelic noun *sinteag*, a noun meaning "leap, jump, bound, stride, skip." *Sinteag* is often used to describe the quick movement of animals and of boats skipping along the water. The pre-eminent Gaelic bard of nature during the eighteenth century, Duncan Bàn Macintyre, described the deer frequenting the mountain Ben Doran:

Leis an eangaig bu chaoile
'S e b' aotruime sìnteag,
Mu chnocanaibh donna ...

With the slenderest small hoof
His stride was the lightest,
All over brown hillocks ...

It can also be found in descriptions of the agile leaps of dancers. In a *port-á-beul* (mouth-music song) describing a dance party, probably from the second half of the eighteenth century, the scene is described vividly:

Sgal air pìoban, sgrìob air fidhlean,
A' cur spìd air calpannan;
Gillean dìreach gearradh shìnteag ...

A blast on the pipes, a scrape on the fiddles,
Causing calves to stir;
Upright boys leaping ...

The chain of associations seems to go something like this: the game of shinny came to be called "shinty" in anglophone Scotland, which

Gaelic speakers associated with the native word *sìnteag*. Not only does *sìnteag* describe the movement of shinty players and the shinty ball itself, but it could also be used to describe the movements of dancers who entertained themselves after the game was over. The word "shinty" thus seems to have gathered a range of associations: quick movement, the racket and fracas of the game and the mêlée surrounding it, and dances held after the game.

The American English "shindig" is even closer in pronunciation to the Gaelic *sìnteag* than it is to "shinty," which suggests the possibility of a direct borrowing from Gaelic-speaking communities, many of which could have brought the ball game and social dancing with them when they settled in North America. Highlanders would have been renowned among their neighbors for throwing the best parties, after all, and if you don't believe that, you deserve a kick to the shins.

Pillion

The noun "pillion" in contemporary English refers to a seat for a passenger behind the driver of a motorcycle. In previous generations, it could also refer to a saddle or cushion for a person seated behind the rider of a horse. "Riding pillion" is a British expression referring to traveling as a passenger on a motorcycle.

The word "pillion" began to appear in Lowland Scots texts in the early sixteenth century: the oldest surviving entries, between 1503 and 1507, describe pillions of gold cloth made for Margaret Tudor, the Queen of Scotland.

"Pillion" is a borrowing of Scottish Gaelic *pillean*, a cushion, padding or saddle made from animal skin. This Gaelic word was adapted from Latin *pellis* "a skin, pelt," an element that can be found in other words in Gaelic, such as *peall* "shaggy hide or skin; couch; covering."

Gaelic aristocrats tended to be keen equestrians and poems in praise of them often mention the showy accoutrements that adorned them and their horses. These are the kinds of fashion statements made in a satirical poem composed in the early eighteenth century that describes the gear on display at the home of a Gaelic warrior:

> 'S iomadh clogaid agus ceannbheart,
> Sgiath amalach dearg is uaine,
> 'S iomadh dìollaid is srian bhuclach,
> Pillean òir is cuirplinn airgid.

> Many helmets and other headgear,
> Many shields with red and green whorls,
> Many saddles and buckled bridles,
> Golden pillions and silver cruppers.

A song composed by Iain Lom MacDonald exults in the defeat of Campbell-led forces at the Battle of Inverlochy in 1645, scorning old rivals for their pomposity and vanity. MacDonald notes with gleeful irony that the flashy paraphernalia of the Campbell élite have become burdens that slow down their escape from their enemies in the fight:

> 'S iomadh fear gòrsaid is pillein,
> cho math 's a bha beò de d' chinneach
> nach d' fhaod a bhòtainn thoirt tioram
> ach foghlam snàmh air bun Nibheis.

Many a fellow with cuirass and pillion,
As fine as ever was in your kindred,
Could not get away with dry boots
But learned to swim in the mouth of the Nevis.

Horses give a sense of freedom and excitement not unlike that of motorcycles, as we can see in this early nineteenth-century praise of a young mare on the Isle of Skye:

A-nis o tha mi 'm aonar
'S gun aon duine cuide rium
Gur teann nach seinn mi ceòl
Air an òg-làir iongantaich;
Nuair bheir mi mach á staball thu
'S a chàireas mi pillean ort
'S leat urram réis na Galltachd,
'S le ceann srian, cha tillear thu ...

Now that I am alone,
Without anyone else nearby,
I cannot help but make music
About the wondrous young mare;
When I take you out of the stable
And I place a pillion on you,
You could take the honor of the Lowland race,
You will not be led home with the bridle ...

Food and Domestic Life

Whisky

The English term "whisky" (spelled "whiskey" in Ireland and the United States) is a borrowing of the Gaelic term *uisge-beatha*, literally meaning "water of life," which is a direct translation of an earlier Latin term. We know that the technique for making whisky had been brought to Gaelic Scotland and Ireland from the continent of Europe by the fifteenth century. One of the chronicles of Ireland records that in 1405 a chieftain "died at Christmas by takeing a surfeit of aqua vitae, to him aqua mortis."

The first appearances of the borrowing in anglophone texts attempt to represent the original Gaelic pronunciation of the word: a collection of Lowland Scots poetry by Robert Sempill, completed in 1583, for example, renders the word as "iskie-bae." Martin Martin gives the spelling "usquebaugh" in his book *A Description of the Western Isles of Scotland*, first printed in 1703. It was not commonly spelled with an initial "w" until the middle of the eighteenth century, by which time the word seems to have become well entrenched in anglophone usage.

It can be difficult to detect the presence of whisky in Gaelic texts because Highland aristocrats preferred wine imported from France and Spain, leaving distilled spirits to the middle classes. Gaelic song-poetry often reflects the values and tastes of the upper classes, obscuring what the lower orders were up to.

A typical song from the seventeenth century, for example, boasts of imbibing wine with the nobles and casts a downward glance at whisky as something belonging not to Highlanders at all but to their loathed Lowland neighbors:

Cha b' e mo dheoch bùrn an fhuarain
No uisge-beatha nan Gall gruamach
Ach fìon dearg a' lìonadh chuachan ...

My drink would not be the water of the spring
nor the whisky of the gloomy Lowlander
but red wine filling the cups.

This is, however, a conceit of the Highland aristocracy rather than a realistic detail that applied to Highland society as a whole. There is a description of a clan gathering in the early eighteenth century in the hall of Simon Fraser of Lovat that reflects the types of drink assigned to each social class:

> As his spacious hall was crowded by kindred visitors, neighbours, vassals, and tenants of all ranks, the table, that extended from one end of it nearly to the other, was covered, at different places, with different kinds of meat and drink; though of each kind there was always great abundance. At the head of the table, the lords and lairds pledged his lordship in claret, and sometimes champagne; the tacksmen, or *daoine uasal*, drank port or whiskey punch; tenants, or common husbandmen, refreshed themselves with strong beer; and below the utmost extent of the table, at the door, and sometimes without the door of the hall, you might see a multitude of Frazers, without shoes or bonnets, regaling themselves with bread and onions, with a little cheese perhaps, and small beer. Yet, amidst the whole of this aristocratical inequality, Lord Lovat had the address to keep all his guests in perfectly good humour. "Cousin," he would say to such and such a tacksman, or *duine uasal*, "I told my pantry lads to hand you some claret, but they tell me ye like port and punch best."

There is a massive amount of lore and practical advice about the consumption of whisky in Gaelic, not to mention song-poetry inspired by it, some of which I collected in my volume *The Naughty Little Book of Gaelic*. A typical example is the guideline about how much to drink:

Aon ghloine: chan fheairrde is cha mhisde e;
Dà ghloine: is fheairrde, is cha mhisde e;
Trì gloineachan: is misde is chan fheairrde e.

One dram: not the better or the worse from it;
Two drams: the better and not the worse from it;
Three drams: the worse and not the better from it.

This sensible advice confirms that, despite the stereotypes of drunken Highlanders, the dangers of drinking to excess were well-known and cautioned against.

It should not be assumed, moreover, that all Highlanders were always unequivocally enthusiastic about whiskey or other types of alcohol. Even back in the mid-1700s, generations before the emergence of the temperance movement, John MacCodrum of North Uist composed a song-poem in the form of a dialog in which two characters - given the names "friend" and "enemy" - engage in a debate over the merits and defects of whisky. It is quite a long piece, and in the middle of the argument, the friend of whisky says:

Nach bòidheach an spòrs
A bhith suidhe mu bhòrdaibh
Le cuideachda chòir
  A bhios an tòir air an dibh!
Bidh mo bhotal air sgòrnan;
A' toirt cop air mo stòpan
Nach toirteil an ceòl leam,

An crònan 's an gliog?

Isn't it a beautiful sport
to be seated among the tables
with a warm-hearted company
    who pursues the drink!
My bottle will be guzzled,
causing my wee flagon to froth;
I certainly find it musical,
    that crooning and burble.

But the enemy of whisky responds in kind:

Nach dona an spòrs
A bhith suidhe mu bhòrdaibh
'S a bhith milleadh mo stòrais
    Le gòraich gun mheas;
Le siaraich 's le stàplaich,
Le briathraibh mì-ghnàthaicht',
Ri speuradh 's ri sàradh
    An Àbharsair dhuibh.

Isn't it an evil sport
to be seated among the tables,
and to be ruining my savings
    with injudicious foolishness;
with staggering and clattering,
with abusive language,
with cursing,
    vexing Satan himself.

It's the critique of drinking culture that gets the last word in the debate, highlighting the financial and physical costs of alcoholism. This hasn't, of course, prevented countless people from indulging and over-indulging in the peat-saturated spirits of Scotland, despite the warnings of poets and priests.

Trews, Trousers

When people think of the clothing of the Scottish Highlands, the first thing that they are likely to think about is the kilt. It may come as a surprise that not only were trousers worn by the male élite of the Gaelic world, but that the word that they had for this garment - *triubhas* - was borrowed into English and eventually evolved into the modern English form "trousers." The Lowland Scots form "trews" is still used and remains closer to the original Gaelic.

References to trews survive in records from the Scottish Lowlands beginning in the sixteenth century, often records of payment that refer to the attire specifically as "Highland trews." Highland clothing became a symbol of the Jacobite cause in the late seventeenth century, giving added significance and symbolism to tartan garments. The idealized iconography of Highland garb remained, especially in literature, long after the defeat at the Battle of Culloden. In his version of a song about the Battle of Sherrifmuir, Robert Burns uses clothing to represent the allegiances of the warriors: "But had you seen the philabegs, and skyrin tartan trews, man ..."

This same Gaelic word made an impression upon English-speaking colonists in Ireland, where they encountered variations of the same clothing at roughly the same time. Shakespeare's play *Henry V*, written in about 1616, has an early example of "trousers," associated specifically with the Gaelic warrior class: "you rode like a Kerne of Ireland, your French Hose off, and in your strait Strossers."

Tight-fitting trews that cover and cushion the crotch are well suited for riding a horse, and horses were largely the privilege of the upper classes and warrior castes of Gaelic society. Trews also took more time and skill to tailor than the long bolts of cloth that were pleated and wound into kilts. Within Gaelic culture itself, then, trews were generally a marker of status and wealth. Poems composed for Highland aristocrats sometimes portray them in this garb. A sixteenth-century Earl of Argyll, for example, is described in his sartorial splendor:

Triobhus donnsróil gun chlaon ccumtha
cuirther uime, móide a mhuirn ...

Well-fitted brown-satin trews
Are put on him, all the better for his cheer ...

Highland trews appear in a number of Gaelic idiomatic expressions.
Chumadh e dha mun do chumadh triubhas dha "It was fitted for him

before trousers were made for him" was a way of implying that something was destined for someone. *Is duilich triubhas a thoirt de mhàs lom* "It's hard to take trousers off of bare buttocks" is said of something futile. *Mar thig triubhas do'n mhuic* "As trousers befit a sow" is said of something that is awkward to do, make or watch.

The words "trews" and *triubhas* are probably encountered most often nowadays in the title of a choreography within the Highland Dancing tradition: *Seann Triubhas* or "Old Trews." The performer, wearing tartan trews, shakes and kicks his legs with great vigor and grace. The usual backstory to the dance is that it represents the dislike of trousers, which were imposed upon Highland men in the aftermath of the failed Jacobite Rising of 1746 and the kilt was banned. This interpretation of the dance is an example of the recent fabrication of tradition, however, rather than accurate historical memory. These technical leg movements were added to the dance in the late nineteenth century by teachers with formal ballet training in order to "improve" it. The idea that these gestures represent the spurning of trousers was only created in the twentieth century. While the dance probably has some origin in a dramatic folk dance from the Highlands in the eighteenth century relating in some way to trousers, it has undergone a radical transformation in style, steps, and meaning.

This short investigation offers a metaphor for how the resources of Gaelic tradition - words, clothing, dance, and so on - have often been appropriated and refashioned by the anglophone world for its own purposes. Perhaps it is time for Highlanders to show that they are not all mouth and no trousers, and to wear the trousers in this relationship again.

Scone

Most bakeries, cafés, and tea shops offer scones with a variety of extra ingredients added to enhance the texture or flavor: raisin scones, chocolate scones, almond scones, potato scones, and so on. The word "scone" was first recorded in Scotland in the early sixteenth century for a much humbler form of sustenance than on offer at the high-end markets of today. The traditional scone can be described as

> A large round cake made of wheat or barley-meal baked on a griddle; one of the four quadrant-shaped pieces into which such a cake is often cut; more generally, a soft cake of barley or oat-meal, or wheat-flour, baked in single portions on a griddle or in an oven.

The early references make it clear that the scone was a rather basic and unassuming staple that was, nonetheless, substantial and nourishing to eat. The word "scone" appears in a number of expressions in Lowland Scots to refer to things that are round, soft, and flat, such as mounds of butter, bonnets, bricks, lumps of cow-dung and people with round faces.

A standard explanation of the origin of the word "scone" is that it is a contraction of the Middle Dutch term *schoonbrot* "fine bread," but William Sayers argued in 2005 that there are problems with this hypothesis. First of all, scones are a rough and ready cake rather than a refined loaf, such as the Dutch term denotes. Secondly, it is odd for an adjective-plus-noun combination ("fine bread") to be shortened to the initial adjective and then borrowed in order to refer to a noun. Finally, it seems unlikely that this type of bread would be imported into Scotland from the continent or that it would have reminded Scots of their own flatbread so much as to borrow the name.

It seems more likely that the term is a borrowing from the Scottish Gaelic noun *sgonn*, which primarily means "lump" or "block," especially of wood, and can be used in reference to other lumpy, chunky or blocky things, including foodstuffs: *sgonn-arain* "lump of bread," *sgonn-gille* "a big lump of a lad," *sgonn-càise* "a chunk of cheese," and so on. This resembles the metaphorical use of "scone" in Lowland Scots. As a verb, Scottish Gaelic *sgonn* means "gulp, glut, eat in large mouthfuls."

A knife handle is described in an early eighteenth-century poem as *sgonn de mhaide seilich* "a chunk of willow wood." A prose sketch of a village game of shinty written in 1848 mentions one of the villagers grabbing *sgonn de dh'isbein* "a lump of sausage." A song composed sometime in the nineteenth century when a local merchant exhibited his first monster cheese in his shop window describes the communal sharing of food at holidays:

Tha 'n Nolluig air tigh'nn teann oirnn,
'S gheibh sinn uile sgonn dhi,
Air bonnach beag 'us toll ann, mar b' àbhaist,
'Us dileag leis do'n Ìleach ...

Christmas is drawing near
And we'll all get a hunk of it,
On a little bannock with a hole in it, as is customary,
And a dram of the Islay malt along with it...

A traditional proverb from Nova Scotia illustrates how song and music were considered to be almost as nourishing as food: *Trì ceathrannan is am fonn, 's math sgonn òrain e* "Three quatrains and the chorus, that's a good chunk of a song."

Bothy

Anyone familiar with hillwalking in Scotland, or with Scottish rural culture in general, will have the word "bothy" in their vocabulary. This term is commonly used for a crude hut or cottage in which people on long treks can take shelter. The Mountain Bothies Association was formed in 1965 to restore abandoned buildings in the countryside so that they can be used by the increasing numbers of people actively walking and climbing over long distances and thus needing some form of overnight accommodation. The majority of the bothies maintained by the organization – over a hundred – are in areas where Gaelic was spoken in the nineteenth century.

The word has also been enshrined in a distinctive genre of Lowland Scottish songs, known as "bothy ballads." Most of the songs in this category were composed by unmarried male farm workers in the north-east of Scotland between 1830 and 1890, housed in a range of lodging arrangements that were generalized with the term "bothy."

"Bothy" has appeared in numerous guises in contemporary popular culture in Scotland and Ireland. *The Bothy Band* was formed in Ireland in 1975 and became one of the most influential groups in the "Celtic music" genre of the era. Scottish musician Martin Bennett released his ground-breaking album *Bothy Culture* in 1998, fusing traditional Highland music with elements from contemporary dance music and a range of world music traditions.

"Bothy" began to appear in written anglophone texts in the eighteenth century to describe Highland shielings, crude shelters used by people who had taken the cattle out to mountain pastures. It appeared increasingly in the nineteenth century to describe other sorts of simple shelters throughout rural Scotland.

The modern word "bothy" is likely to have mixed parentage, a convergence of words in both Gaelic and Germanic languages with similar sounds and meanings. The Gaelic terms *bothan* and *bothag* are diminutive forms of the noun *both*, primarily meaning a hut or cabin. The Lowland Scots term "buith," a covered stall or a small enclosed shelter, is related to English "booth," both derived from the Old Norse word *boþ*. The resemblance between these Gaelic and Germanic words enabled them to mingle and merge on the tongues of Scots.

The Gaelic term *both* features in many different place names in Scotland, such as Bocastle (originally *Both Chaisteil* "Hut of the Castle," near Callander), Balquidder (originally *Both Phuidir*), Boquhapple (originally *Both a' Chapaill* "Hut of the Horse," near Thornhill), Boath (originally *na Bothachan* "the places of huts," in Ross), and Bohuntin (*Both Chunndainn* "Hut of the Confluence," in Glenroy).

There are many traditional Gaelic songs by women reminiscing about blissful summers spent with the cattle on the mountain grazings, sleeping at night in the bothy, and often visited by sweethearts. One of the best known of these compositions, known by the title *Bothan Àirigh am Bràighe Raineach* ("The Shieling Hut on the Braes of Rannoch"), was likely composed in the late seventeenth century and depicts an idyllic pastoral life:

Ann am bothan an t-sùgraidh

Is gur e bu dùnadh dha barrach.
Bhiodh a' chuthag 's an smùdan
A' gabhail ciùil duinn air chrannaibh.
Bhiodh an damh donn 's a' bhùireadh
Gar dùsgadh 's a' mhadainn.

In the bothy of courtship
Closed over with brushwood;
With the cuckoo and ring-dove
Singing in the branches,
And the brown rutting stag
Arousing us at morning.

Pet

A pet is domesticated animal kept primarily for human companionship, rather than the production of food or other forms of exploitation. It can also refer to a person who is pampered or treated with special partiality, like a favorite child or student. It makes four brief appearances in sixteenth-century Lowland Scottish literature, three of which refer to cats as the familiar of witches ("carling's pet"). It resurfaces more widely in seventeenth-century anglophone texts, with a particular association with sheep.

The original researchers of the *Oxford English Dictionary*, who completed their work by 1910, did not propose a history of the word. Some scholars suggested that it was a shortened borrowing of French *petit* into English, or that it was acquired through wordplay from Old French *pet* "fart." These desperate speculations persisted for decades after the accomplished Irish scholar Thomas F. O'Rahilly demonstrated that the word had in fact been borrowed into English from Gaelic.

The noun *peata* "domesticated animal" can be traced back to the seventh century in native sagas and law tracts. Parts of the great epic *Táin Bó Cuailgne* were written as early as the eighth century and in one of the mini-stories that preface it, about how the boy-warrior Cú Chulainn took up his weapons, the company sees a herd of deer. Cú Chulainn asked if they were pets or if they were wild deer (*pettai sút no inn aigi chena*). Then they see a flock of wild swans, and Cú Chulainn asked if they were pets or wild birds (*Indat pettai sút no indat éoin chena*).

Many Celtic saints are depicted as having animal companions in the early lives written about them. The most common pets mentioned in early Gaelic texts are cats, dogs, and herons, but other native animals kept as companions are also mentioned. Early Gaelic laws dealing with the mutual rights and duties of neighboring farmers provided guidelines in the case that damage was done by pet wolves, foxes, deer, or herons. There are also occasional references to much more exotic pets as well: King Edgar of Scotland sent a pet camel to Muirchertach Úa Briain of Ireland in the year 1105.

The word *peata* even developed the connotation of "pampered thing" by the early seventeenth century. The Irish poet and Catholic priest Geoffrey Keating (*c*.1569-*c*.1644), who trained in the Irish College in Bordeuax, France, before returning to serve in Ireland, stated *saoghal peata ní mheasaim ... do bheith agam* "I do not expect to have a pampered life."

The English etymologists who assumed that *peata* could not be a borrowing from Gaelic objected on the basis that the word starts with the letter "p," which the ancestral Celtic language had discarded in the prehistoric period. The Brythonic branch of Celtic, however, reacquired the sound in the Iron Age, and this was the variety of Celtic spoken throughout Britain when the Romans invaded, surviving down to the present day in Wales, Cornwall, and Brittany. There are many loanwords from Brythonic Celtic languages that came into the Gaelic of

Ireland and especially of Scotland. Some of this is due to centuries of co-existence and interaction between Brythonic and Gaelic speakers, but also because the native peoples of Scotland who had originally spoken a Brythonic language – especially those commonly but simplistically referred to as "Picts" – were largely assimilated into Gaelic society but retained some elements of their language and culture.

Gaelic *peata* "domesticated animal" is related to Welsh *peth* "thing, possession; portion, quantity." Another link in the chain of evidence about this linguistic borrowing from Brythonic into Scottish Gaelic is the place name element "pit" which can be found all around central and north eastern Scotland in such place names as Pitlochry, Pitcarmick, Pitgaveny, and Pittenweem. This place name element is recorded as *pett* in the Gaelic notes written in the twelfth century in the Book of Deer from Aberdeenshire. As Scottish place name scholar Simon Taylor notes:

> *Pett* no doubt had a well-defined function as a term describing a land-holding unit within the Pictish kingdom, and was adopted into Scottish Gaelic as part of the administrative system inherited by Alba from its Pictish predecessor. If we accept that *pett* was part of the lexicon of north-east Scotland in the early centuries of Scottish Gaelic, then we must seriously consider the possibility that it is being used as a common noun in the property-records in the Book of Deer.

The common thread between the diverging developments of the words *pett / peata / peth* is ownership and possession: some general thing owned by a person, an animal claimed by a person as a companion, and an estate occupied and organized by people.

The word *peata* can be found in several prominent Scottish Gaelic texts from the early modern period. One of the novice compositions by Jacobite poet Alasdair mac Mhaighstir Alasdair in the early eighteenth century, perhaps an exercise in parody, is called *Marbhrann do pheata coluim* "Elegy to a pet dove."

One of the many folktales collected in the mid-nineteenth century by the team of fieldworkers coordinated by John Francis Campbell is called *Am Peata Bàn* "The White Pet." The tale begins when a lamb - the white pet of the title - heard that its master was contemplating slaughtering it for a Christmas meal. It decides to escape to avoid this unsavory fate and encounters other domesticated animals owned by the farmer – a bull, a dog, a cat, a cock, and a goose – all of whom want to evade being butchered and so join the lamb's get-away plan.

Am Peata Bàn is a Gaelic variant of a story told in many other languages and cultures, but whatever the ultimate origins of the folktale, it reflects human self-awareness of the exploitations of animals and the many kinds of burdens born by them for human interests. It likely had its greatest resonance among people on the the lowest rungs of the social ladder who felt similarly "fleeced" by the élite.

Caber

A caber is a long, straight, roughly-hewn tree trunk, typically used as rafters or beams in houses and other buildings. Highland Games are often characterized, tongue-in-cheek, as festivals where large men in kilts throw heavy objects – most especially the caber. "Tossing the caber," as it is traditionally called in English, involves lifting a tree trunk some 20 feet long, weighing about 12.5 stones (equivalent to 175 pounds or 79 kilograms). The contestant then moves forward with it and launches it into the air in order for it for turn a somersault and come to rest on the ground pointing straight ahead.

The first record of this trial of strength is in the chronicles of the Frasers recording a festive gathering in Strathglass in 1655 that included "jumping, arching, shooting, throwing the barr, the stone, and all manner of manly exercise imaginable ..." There were practical reasons for cultivating strength and the ability to handle large timber: such skills were needed for building the roofs of traditional houses, and while many areas of the Highlands have been barren for a long time, expert foresters have managed woodlands for many centuries in some places, especially in the central Highlands.

The noun "caber" began to appear in Lowland Scots documents by the early sixteenth century to refer to wood and timber resources, clearly accepted as a standard term of reference for building supplies.

The Lowland Scots noun "caber" is a borrowing of the Gaelic *cabar* with exactly the same sense of "pole, rafter, tree trunk." It is also the word used in Gaelic for horns or antlers. Those familiar with Highland musical tradition will recognize the words *Cabar Féidh* (meaning "Deer Antlers") in the title of a Gaelic song and a reel (or march) for the bagpipe or fiddle. Both of these are associated with the MacKenzies, whose heraldic emblem is the stag.

The Gaelic song has a very complicated history but begins with the 1715 Jacobite Rising, when the MacKenzies fought for the exiled Stuart kings. The author of the song praises the chieftain of the MacKenzies of Seaforth using the symbolism of the majestic and fierce stag, with obvious phallic overtones:

Cha deach Cataich air an tapadh:
Dh'fhàg an neart le eagal iad

Ri faicinn ceann an fhéidh ort
Nuair dh'éirich do chabar ort.

Sutherland men performed no exploits:
Their strength deserted them in fright
At seeing the deer's head on you
When your antlers rose up over you.

The song was highly popular in the Highlands and the melody was adapted for the Highland bagpipes and adopted by the MacKenzies. It is often referred to as their "clan march." Since then the tune has undergone many transformations and become popular on the fiddle and in Irish tradition as well. The tune is frequently played to accompany Highland Dancing.

The word *cabar* occurs in many place names across Scotland, such as Cabrach in Aberdeenshire and Cabrich near Inverness. It also appears in an amusing Gaelic expression: *Cuir sìoda air cabar is bidh e brèagha* "Put silk on a caber and it will be lovely," meaning "All show and no substance."

Ingle

The noun "ingle" refers to an open fire in a domestic space, such as in a fireplace or hearth. It came into the wider English vocabulary from Lowland Scots, where it first appears in the early sixteenth century. Gavin Douglas translated Virgil's *Aeneid* into Lowland Scots in 1513 and refers to sacred fires and funeral pyres with the word "ingill." Robert Burns also used the word in his popular poem "The Cotter's Saturday Night," published in 1786, which helped to spread it to a wider audience.

"Ingle" is a borrowing of the Scottish Gaelic *aingeal*, which means "angel; fire; light." The poet Iain Lom MacDonald used *aingeal* for a fire that could be used for cooking in a poem from about 1685. When Edward Lhuyd toured the Highlands collecting words and manuscripts for his research at the end of the seventeenth century, he transcribed two phrases meaning "light a fire," both of which used the word *aingeal*.

This word seems to have become much less commonly used in the eighteenth century, although Argyllshire poet Duncan Bàn Macintyre used it of the flint spark that fired his gun in songs he composed from the mid-eighteenth to early nineteenth centuries.

Nineteenth-century folklorist Alexander Carmichael was quite aware that the word "ingle" was a borrowing from Gaelic, as he tells us in notes in his celebrated volumes *Carmina Gadelica*: "*Aingeal* meaning fire is current in some districts though obsolete in others. The word is borrowed into Scots and applied to the hearth, as 'ingle' ..."

The image of relaxing, warm and cozy, by the fireside on a winter's night has appeared in many poems that have invoked the word "ingle." One such is "Fancy," by John Keats, composed in 1819:

Sit thee by the ingle, when
The sear faggot blazes bright,
Spirit of a winter's night; ...

Landscape and Nature

Bog

Over twenty percent of the land surface of Scotland is covered by bogs, and ninety percent of those bogs are classified as blanket bogs. Bogs are particularly common in the landscape of the traditionally Gaelic-speaking Highlands and Western Isles. Peat cut from bogs were a key source of fuel for heating, and the walls and thatch of some traditional buildings incorporated turf. The soil of the peat bogs gives Scotch whisky its unique flavor.

It is no surprise, then, that English speakers would have borrowed a word from Gaelic for a feature that is so widespread in the Scottish Highlands and Ireland. This unique ecosystem has also provided colorful idioms and expressions in English, often with negative connotations, such as "getting bogged down." In modern Lowland Scots, "boggin" is an adjective meaning "dirty, smelly, revolting."

One of the first appearances of the word "bog" in English is in a poem by the Lowland Scots poet William Dunbar, addressed to Queen Margaret Tudor of Scotland, who married King James IV in 1503. The term was used in political and geographical accounts of Ireland and Highland Scotland in the sixteenth and seventeenth centuries, and was further adopted by writers such as Shakespeare, Robert Burns, and Walter Scott.

The word *bog* in Scottish Gaelic is a noun signifying "bog, marsh." There are two further words in Gaelic based on the root element *bog* that are used commonly of bogs, marshes, and fens: *bogach* and *boglach*.

Bog is also an adjective meaning "soft; boggy; damp, water-logged." A misty day in Gaelic is *latha bog*. *Bog* is used as an intensifier with *fliuch* "wet" to describe something that is soggy: *Tha sin bog fliuch* "That is totally drenched."

Wetlands such as bogs are natural carbon sinks, absorbing much more carbon dioxide than forests in Europe. Bogs deserve more respect than they've been given by anglophones in the past. Maybe a better understanding of Gaelic can help with that.

Crag

The noun "crag," meaning "a large, jagged rock or cliff" and the related adjective "craggy" have been in mainstream use by English speakers for a long time, especially by those living in or near areas where speakers of Celtic languages had been the dominant inhabitants.

"Crag" (or similar forms such as "kragge" and "craig") began to appear in anglophone texts in Scotland in the fourteenth century and was in mainstream Lowland usage by the eighteenth century. John Macky, a Scot living in England in the eighteenth century, tells us as much in a letter written in the 1720s describing the landscape around Kirkcudbright:

> ... a rocky stony Crest, which in this Country they call Crags, for they make a distinction here between Mountains, Hills, and Crags. ... The Crags are hard stony Rocks, not high, and thinly cover'd with Grass, through which the Rocks appear like a Scab.

"Crag" is derived from Scottish Gaelic *creag* of exactly this meaning. It appears in place names all around Scotland, some of which are attached to very well known locations or features of the landscape. The Salisbury Crags jut up near Arthur's Seat in Hollyrood Park near the Scottish Parliament in Edinburgh and were known in the twelfth century by the Gaelic name *Creag nam Marbh* "The Crags of the Dead." Ailsa Craig is an island off of the shore of Ayrshire formed by a volcanic plug that has been the source for curling stones since the mid-nineteenth century.

The surname Craig was derived in multiple locations in Scotland from place names that included this element. Johannes del Crag was one of the witnesses of a charter during the reign of William the Lion (1142-1214) and by the fifteenth century there were three different unrelated families who styled themselves with this surname. There is a slew of other surnames in Lowland Scotland based on place names that include "crag," sometimes incorporating other Gaelic elements, such as Craigforth, Craigie, Craigingelt, and Craigmillar.

Perhaps it is fitting that a country famed for its rough mountains and hard men to have contributed this word to English, and for it to be the surname (after inserting an -i-) of the most recent actor to play that iconic tough-guy with Scottish ancestry: James Bond.

Loch

One of the Gaelic words known by most anglophones is *loch*, given that it can be found in the names of so many bodies of fresh water in Scotland, from Loch Ness to Loch Lomond. Loch Lomond is the largest inland body of water on the island of Britain and there are many thousands more, small and large, around Scotland which bear the Gaelic word *loch* in their names.

It is often claimed that there is only natural fresh-water body in Scotland whose name uses "lake" rather than "loch" - the Lake of Menteith - but even this is misleading. It is known in Gaelic as *Loch Innse Mo Cholmaig* "The lake of the island of Saint Colmag" and it was only given the name "the Lake of Menteith" in English at the beginning of the nineteenth century! The word "loch" is a Gaelic word that truly spans Scotland's landscape.

The place name element "loch" has frequently appeared in anglophone literature and in the titles of poems, books, songs, and music groups, such as Lord Byron's "Loch na Garr," the folk song "The Bonny Banks of Loch Lomond," Walter Scott's poem "Lochinvar" and the Scottish folk band The Lochies.

Water - in the form of glaciers, rivers, floods, and tides - has moulded the landscape of Scotland over many millennia. There is a specific logic in Gaelic place names - often inherited from the earlier Brythonic-speaking peoples - that associates the names of rivers with some of the the natural features made by or related to them spatially, including lochs, as the Gaelic scholar William J. Watson explained:

> In Celtic nomenclature, the river regularly gives its name to the loch whence it issues, the strath, glen, or corry through which it flows, and the place where it falls into the sea or another stream. The loch is regarded as the reservoir of the river ... This (consistent pattern) is of great importance in dealing with names of lochs, straths, and glens.

Highland folklore manifests the mysteries and dangers of lochs in the form of the *each-uisge* "water horse." Adomnán's biography of Saint Columba of Iona, written in the late seventh century, contains the earliest surviving account of such an aquatic monster. In this episode, Columba had been in Pictish territory for some time and after crossing the river Ness, came across people burying a man who had been killed by a monster as he was swimming in the loch. The holy man commanded that one of his own followers swim across to the opposite bank of the loch to get a boat, knowing that the beast would notice the movement in the water. As the monk was half-way across the loch, the beast rose to the surface with a roar and opened its muzzle to feast on the man, but the saint intervened just before it could get its next meal, commanding it to stop and return to its lair. According to Adomnán, this miracle allowed Columba to demonstrate the superior power of the Christian God and the Picts responded with awe and devotion, as he had wished.

This was, of course, the debut of the Loch Ness monster in written form, but she has cousins all across the Highlands who have inspired horror stories repeated around the peat fire for many centuries. As the Gaelic folklorist John Gregorson Campbell noted in the nineteenth century,

> The belief in the existence of the water-horse is now in the Highlands generally a thing of the past, but in olden times almost every lonely freshwater lake was tenanted by one – sometimes by several – of these animals.

> In shape and colour it resembled an ordinary horse, and was often mistaken for one. It was seen passing one lake to another, mixing with the farmers' horses in the adjoining pastures, and waylaid belated travellers who passed near its haunts. It was highly dangerous to touch or mount it. Those whom it decoyed into doing so were taken away to the loch in which it had its haunt, and there devoured. It was said to make its approaches also in other guises – as a young man, a boy, a ring, and even a tuft of wool (*ribeag clòimhe*); and any woman upon whom it set its mark was certain at last to become its victim.

"Loch" has sometimes also been used in the names of places far away from Scotland to give them an "Old World" aura, as has other name elements derived from Gaelic, such as glen, strath, ben, kyle, dun, and so on. There are communities named "Loch Lomond" in the states of Florida and Virginia within the United States, for example.

An artificial reservoir in North Carolina, originally christened "Lake Norman," is referred to as "Loch Norman" by those who organize a local Scottish Highland Games nearby. Like Loch Ness, whose water beast is usually called "Nessie" in English, rumors began to circulate in 1996 of a supernatural denizen of Lake Norman named "Normie."

Whether this is due to the migration of amphibians, a marketing stunt, or the influence of whisky, the word "loch" reminds us of the universal allure of the mysteries of the depths of dark waters.

Dulse

Dulse, whose Latin species name is *palmaria palmata,* is a variety of seaweed that resembles leafy red lettuce. Food researchers have become excited about dulse in recent years because it's not only rich in fiber, protein, vitamins, trace, fatty acids, and antioxidants, it even tastes like bacon when it is fried! Who would have expected that the next superfood would come from the humble diet of Gaels living along the shores of the Atlantic for generations beyond memory?

One of the earliest records of the English word "dulse" comes from the writings of Martin Martin, a native Gael from the Isle of Skye who compiled an account of the Western Isles of Scotland in the late seventeenth century. Martin made many observations about the ways in which islanders made use of the natural resources available to them. His chapter about how the people of Skye harvested seaweed contains a fascinating description of dulse and how it was used to cure constipation, poor eyesight, headaches, worms, and other ailments:

> Dulse is a reddish brown colour, about ten or twelve inches long, and above half an inch in breadth: it is eat raw, and then reckon'd to be loosening, and very good for the Sight; but if boil'd, it proves more loosening, if the Juice be drank with it. The Plant apply'd Plaister-wise to the Temples, is reckon'd effectual against the Megrim: the Plant boil'd and eat with its Infusion, is used against the Cholick and Stone; and dry'd without washing it in water, pulveriz'd and given in any convenient Vehicle fasting, it kills Worms: the Natives eat it boil'd with Butter, and reckon it very wholesome. The Dulse recommended here, is that which grows on Stone, and not that which grows on the Alga Marina, or Sea-Tangle; for tho that be likewise eaten, it will not serve in any of the Cases above mention'd.

Rare early records of folk remedies such as these confirm that people have creatively experimented with the properties of plants and carefully observed their effects on living beings and their afflictions for a very long time.

Dulse has been an essential ingredient in many medicinal recipes documented in Gaeldom's seaside communities over the last two centuries. It has also been used to induce a sweat, relieve digestive problems, plaster wounds of the flesh, reduce fever, and expel afterbirth.

The English noun "dulse" is derived from the Gaelic word *duileasg*.
References to it, especially in the writings of natural historians,

increased in the eighteenth century. It was noted in the nineteenth century that the Gaels chewed on dulse as a matter of habit but that an American import was replacing dulse with detrimental results: dulse "was much eaten by the Highlanders till it was supplanted by that nauseous herb, tobacco; and well would it have been for both purse and person, if they had continued to prefer it to a costly narcotic."

One of the earliest appearances of the word in Gaelic is in a poem in the voice of the sixth-century churchman Saint Columba, although the text was actually composed in the twelfth century. The poem expresses the delight of a simple, solitary, self-sufficient life devoted to God on the island of Iona on the west coast of Scotland:

Seal ag buain duilisg do charraig,
 seal ar aclaidh,
seal ag tabhairt bhídh do bhochtaibh,
 seal i gcarcair.

A while plucking dulse from the skerries,
 a while fishing,
a while giving food to the needy,
 a while in a rock-cell.

Carrageen (also known as "Irish moss") is another species of seaweed known in English by its Gaelic name and harvested for a variety of medicinal and dietary purposes. A traditional rhyme offers advice on the best times to harvest the main varieties of seaweed used by Gaelic communities:

Cairgean earraich
Duileasg samhraidh,
Gruaigean foghair,
Stamh geamhraidh.

Spring carrageen
Summer dulse
Autumn badderlocks
Winter oarweed.

Gaelic folklore contains an abundance of valuable information and practical guidance, as well as entertainment. Whether or not you wish to spend the rest of your days on a remote island plucking dulse from rocks in the sea is up to you!

Ptarmigan

The ptarmigan is a variety of grouse found in northern regions of Eurasia and North America. Its feathers, which cover its feet, turn from brown or grey in the summer to white in the winter. It is shy and skittish by nature, and its cooing can often be heard before it can be seen in the high, remote ascents of the Highlands.

The ptarmigan is the official bird of the territory of Nunavut in Canada. Its name appears in many places in North America, such as Ptarmigan Peak in Colorado (US), Ptarmigan Traverse in Washington State (US), Ptarmigan Peak in Alberta (Canada) and Ptarmigan Creek Provincial Park in British Columbia (Canada). There are also several bodies of water named "Ptarmigan Lake" in the United States and Canada.

The name of this bird was borrowed from Scottish Gaelic *tarmachan* (also known in variants *tàrmachan* and *tormachan*) into Lowland Scots in the sixteenth century in forms such as "tarmagan" and "termigan." It is likely based on the Gaelic word *torm(an)* meaning "murmur." The bird's Gaelic name is thus likely to refer to the loud cooing and murmuring noises that it makes.

Despite inhabiting mountain peaks far from human habitation, Gaels were familiar enough with them and their behavior to refer to them in common expressions. It was said, for example, *Cha chuir fuachd no acras an tarmachan gu srath* "Neither cold nor hunger will drive the ptarmigan to a strath," which could be used to allude to the personality of people as well, introverts in particular. *Cha tachair siud gus an tig an tarmachan do thaigh nan cearc* "That will not happen until the ptarmigan comes to the hen-house" was akin to saying, "Not until Hell freezes over."

In 1684 Robert Sibbald, a pioneering scholar and native of Edinburgh, published a volume of natural history focusing on Scotland entitled *Scotia Illustrata*. He inserted the letter "p" at the beginning of the name of this bird on the mistaken assumption that it was derived from Greek! This form of the word was then brought into English by the naturalist Thomas Pennant from Sibbald's text in the late eighteenth century.

The ptarmigan appears in Gaelic songs of praise to hunters as a symbol emphasizing the strength and agility needed to reach its native habitat and pursue it successfully. It also appears in Gaelic literature describing the flora and fauna of the Highlands for their own sake.

An ode to the season of summer composed by Archibald Campbell of St. Fillans, Loch Earn-side, in the early nineteenth century mentions them among others:

Bithidh na lachai' gu cuannar
Air na feur-lochain uain' a' snàmh;
Is pairt dhiubh 's an luachair,
Gabhail fasgaidh taobh bhruachan nan allt;
'S bithidh na tarmachain bhreaca
Air na stùchdan fo stachdan nam beann;
Seirmeadh an crònan le taitneas
'S b' e mo shòlas bhith dearc' os an ceann.

The wild ducks elegantly
Float on the green, reedy lakes;
Some of them are in the rushes,

Taking shelter in the banks of the burns;
And the dappled ptarmigans
Are on the pinnacles under the mountain peaks;
Let them croon with delight
It is my joy to watch them from above.

Slang and Idioms

Galore

The word "galore," meaning "plenty, in abundance," is one of the most obvious borrowings from Gaelic into English. It is one of the few adjectives or adverbs in English to follow the Gaelic pattern of coming at the end of a phrase: we generally say "whisky galore," for example, rather than "galore whisky."

The phrase *gu leòr* has the exact same meaning in Gaelic and is found in both Irish and Scottish branches of the language. It seems to begin to appear in English texts in the late seventeenth century, such as in an entry from 1675 in the diary of Henry Teonge, an English chaplain in the Royal Navy.

It is hard to be certain whether these early and sporadic occurrences are due to Irish or Scottish influence, but it is noteworthy that borrowings begin to appear in Lowland Scots texts in the mid-eighteenth century, with various spellings, such as "gilore" and "gelore." Its adoption into mainstream English is therefore as likely to come from Scottish Gaelic as Irish.

Grotty, Grody

"Grotty" started to appear in British slang in the early 1960s, especially in youth culture. The *Oxford English Dictionary* quotes the spectator of a hockey game in 1964 calling the match "grotty," while the 1966 novel *Cork on the Telly*, set in London, used the word to describe the sound of corrupted audio recordings. Poorly cleaned houses and pubs were also being described as "grotty" in the same time frame.

A close variant of the word began to crop up in the youth slang of the United States in the 1980s with the spelling "grody." This word probably got its maximum exposure in the 1982 song "Valley Girl" by Frank Zappa and his daughter Moon Unit. The Zappas intended the song to be a parody of the way that trendy teenage girls of San Fernando Valley of California spoke. A section of the lyrics read:

> It's, like, so bitchin', 'cause, like, everybody's, like,
> Super-super nice,
> It's, like, so bitchin' ...
> So, like, I go into this, like, salon place, you know,
> And I wanted, like, to get my toenails done,
> And the lady, like, goes, oh my God, your toenails
> Are, like, so grody;
> It was, like, really embarrassing ...

The standard authorities derive both "grotty" and "grody" from "grotesque," but Gaelic offers a better match both in terms of sound and sense: *grod* "rotten, putrid; corrupt." This word can be traced back to Gaelic texts of the early medieval period with the meanings "bitter, musty, rotten" and was commonly used of food, plants, and other organic matter that decays.

Besides food, one of the most common items to be described as *grod* in Scottish Gaelic is wood, but even stone structures could be described as such. In an anecdote printed in 1876 about the Jacobite army's march into England in 1745, the effect of a siege on Carlisle was said to cause the walls of the garrison to become *grod* "decayed, ruinous."

There are numerous examples of its usage in modern Scottish Gaelic in metaphorical rather than strictly literal, physical senses. In a letter written in 1901 to the editor of the all-Gaelic periodical *Mac-Talla*, printed in Nova Scotia, Canada, for example, a reader urges young people to resist the allure of the anglophone world and stay true to their Highland heritage. He begins by mocking what he saw as the naive capitulation of the youth:

"Leanamaid cleachdaidhean gallda, fasana gallda 's iad cho brèagha." Brèagha ach grod, is e tha mis' ag innseadh dhuibh: freagraidh iad ann an tomhas do na Gaill ach cha fhreagair do na Gàidheil, ma tha 'd déidheil air bhi nan daoine treun, glan, calma agus onarach 's nan caileagan 's nam mnathan glan, fallainn agus eireachdail.

"Let's adopt non-Gaelic customs, non-Gaelic fashions, as they are so charming." Charming but rotten, is what I tell you: they are appropriate to a degree for non-Gaels but they are not appropriate for the Gaels, if they are eager to be strong, uncorrupted, brave and honorable, and the girls to be uncorrupted, healthy and beautiful.

The opposition drawn out in this text, similar to others in Gaelic, is between the words *grod* "repulsive, rotten, corrupt" and *glan* "clean, pure, upstanding." Perhaps if that Valley Girl had followed that sound Gaelic advice, she might have kept her toes cleaner and avoided embarrassing herself?

Gob

"Gob" is a well-established slang term referring to the mouth, usually with mocking, sarcastic, or humorous overtones. It is used in modern British idioms such as "gob-smacked" (to be astonished), "gobstopper" (hard candy) and "gobshite" (a loud-mouthed or indiscreet person).

Although it is commonly assumed that "gob" is a late borrowing from Irish, it has actually been in use in Lowland Scots since at least the sixteenth century. It entered northern English dialects by the late seventeenth century and the street-slang of London by the mid-nineteenth century.

The Lowland Scots word was borrowed from the Scottish Gaelic *gob*, which refers primarily to the beak of a bird. It is also used of the human mouth, with similar overtones of mockery, sarcasm, or humor. A common Gaelic admonition used by adults to silence a child is *Dùin do ghob!* "Shut your beak!"

Another example of using the part of an animal to refer to the corresponding part of a human body occurs in the Gaelic word *spòg*. It refers most specifically to the paw of an animal, but can also be used for the human hand. Gaelic *spòg* was also borrowed into Lowland Scots as "spag" (variants "spaag," "spague," "spyaug," and "spaig") with the same nuances.

Gob is used metaphorically in Gaelic for things that resemble beaks and mouths. *Gob-dubhain* is the end of a fishing hook and *gob-claidheimh* is the point of a sword. *Gob* is also used of the end-point of landscape features and can be found in such place names as *Gob na h-Éist* "Neist Point" on the Isle of Skye and *Gob na Cananaich* "Chanonry Point" on the Black Isle between Fortrose and Rosemarkie.

Gob appears in Gaelic adages that comment on human failings and flaws. All talk and no action? In Gaelic, that's *Gob mór, ugh beag* "Big mouth, little egg."

Cosy, Cozy

The word "cosy" (spelled "cozy" in American English) is an adjective describing the state of being warm, snug, and comfortable, like a blanket wrapped around you on a winter's night. A tea cosy is a thick cloth covering made to fit tightly over a teapot so that it will retain its heat.

The earliest surviving instances of "cosy" are in Lowland Scots literature of the early eighteenth century, used to describe people and places. "Cozy" began to enter mainstream English usage in the mid-eighteenth century but it was especially through the poetry of Robert Burns in the late eighteenth century that the word gained widespread acceptance. In his celebrated poem "To a Mouse," composed in 1785 and published the next year, Burns finds a mouse in its nest where it is sheltering from the wintery weather: "An' cozie here, beneath the blast, Thou thought to dwell..."

Etymologists have not yet agreed upon an origin for the word. One suggestion is that is derived from a Northern Germanic word related to the modern Norwegian *koseleg*, meaning essentially "enjoyable, nice, comfortable." This does not, however, provide the physical connotations of warm, snugness, and shelter implied by "cosy." In 1887, Walter Skeat proposed that it was derived from the Gaelic root *còs*, a proposal which is worth pursuing by examining usages and meanings in Gaelic.

By itself, *còs* means "hole, cave, cavity, hollow"; *còsach* is the adjectival form, meaning primarily "full of holes or cavities" but also carrying the secondary meanings of "snug; spongy, porous." There are two diminutive forms of *còs* - *còsag* and *còsan* - and these have corresponding adjectival forms with the same meanings, although *còsagach* was also recorded as having the explicit secondary meanings of "snug, warm, cosy, sheltered" (as well as "spongy").

An example can help to explain how the Gaelic term correlates to the English word. In his book describing Canada for potential Highland emigrants, published in 1841, Robert McDougall provides copious observations about the culture and customs of First Nations. In a passage about native hunting practices, he describes how a hunter would be encased in a hollow tree and wait until he could spring upon unsuspecting animals:

> *Aithnichidh iad an t-àite de'n choille bhios na féidh a' taoghal, agus 'nuair a thachras iad ri àite de'n t-seòrsa sin, ballaichidh iad air craoibh chòsaich, claghaichidh iad toll innt' air am faigh fear-amais math a-staigh ...*

> They will identify the place in the forest that the deer frequent, and when they come across a place of that sort, they will mark a holed tree, (and) they will hollow open a cavity in it into which a good marksman can get inside ...

In this passage, a tree is chosen on the basis of having a good internal space, which is further emptied out, creating a snug chamber for the hunter. The Gaelic term *còs(ag)* is a place where a being can find warm, snug shelter - like a mouse in its nest.

Snazzy

The English adjective "snazzy" connotes someone or something whose appearance is stylish, elegant, classy, or flashy. It became common in American English in the 1930s. The *Oxford English Dictionary* lists two appearances in sources from California, as well as a mention in a dictionary of underworld and prison slang collected in the United States in that decade. A definitive explanation for the origin of the word has been elusive and it may be that it has multiple parentage.

The Gaelic noun *snas* implies the same set of qualities: "perfection; a comely appearance; elegance, polish." The adjectival form is *snasta* or *snasail* and is a very common compliment that can be traced in Gaelic texts back to the early medieval period. A fourteenth-century poet anticipating a raid by Eòin MacSuibhne to retake Castle Sween in Knapdale describes each soldier sporting *stargha snasta suairc* "a snazzy, handsome shield." The second poem in Alasdair mac Mhaighstir Alasdair's 1751 self-published volume of poetry is an invocation of the Muses, in which he asks them to *Locair gu snasta gach siolladh d'am chainnt* "Make snazzy every syllable of my speech."

A simple Gaelic pedigree is complicated by the counter claim that the slang term was based on the nickname of a popular performer at the turn of the twentieth century, the opera singer George Harry Snazel (1848-1912), who went by the stage-name Mr G. H. Snazelle. By the early twentieth century, he was sometimes referred to as "Snazzy," as evidenced by newspaper articles from Wellington, New Zealand in 1901 and Dunedin, New Zealand in 1903.

While the idea that the nickname for the opera singer may have led to the slang term has attracted some attention, there are some problems with this explanation. First of all, the gap between his death (1912) and the first appearance of the adjective (in the 1930s) is too long and silent. Secondly, there is no evidence that Snazel's appearance or persona were uniquely elegant enough – beyond other performers of his type in his era – to earn a reputation that would lead to the creation of a popular word based on his name.

Mass media – newspapers, radio, and films – were increasingly present and influential in the lives of anglophones in the 1930s, when "snazzy" began to circulate widely. Words catch on for strange and unpredictable reasons, seemingly from nowhere, and mass media broadcast these coinages quickly to widespread audiences. There is a small collection of American slang from this era of unknown origin that end in "-zz" or "-zzy," such as jazz, tizzy, doozy, woozy, and floozy. Gaelic origins have been proposed for some of these. It may be that *snas* was remolded by the shape of this street talk when it began to jostle with other slang in the media centers and immigrant communities of California, where the first records of its use were noted.

There were Scottish Gaelic speakers in urban centers along the west coast of North America in the early twentieth century who made efforts to maintain and promote their native language. Some of them were also noted for sporting tartans and kilts: Highland Games had taken root in the San Francisco Bay area by 1869 and gained popularity throughout the nineteenth century. A letter to a Scottish periodical submitted by a Highland immigrant in San Francisco in 1907 portrays this tartan swagger:

Tha Seumas Sinclair agus na Gàidheil eile anns a' bhaile gu math. Bidh Seumas gu tric a' spaidsearachd anns an deise Ghaidhealach le chlaidheamh air a shliasaid ach cha bhi e deanamh cron sam bith air na Goill ged nach toil leis iad.

James Sinclair and the other Gaels in the city are doing well. James frequently struts around the city in Highland clothing with his sword at his side, but he does not do any harm to the non-Gaels, even though he doesn't like them.

Perhaps snazzily dressed Highland immigrants, playing up tartan stereotypes, helped to promote the image that had already been popularized by the rise of Highland Games during the Victorian Era as well as popular celebrities such as Harry Lauder. The success of *Outlander* in the present day demonstrates that this sartorial splendor continues to win hearts.

Brash

The first known appearance of the word "brash" is in a book published in 1824 to illustrate a local dialect in Yorkshire, England. It is used twice in dialog spoken by a woman named Bridget. "Brash" is defined in a glossary in this book as meaning "impetuous, rash."

The next appearance is in the Gothic novel *Nick of the Woods; or, The Jibbenainesay,* published in 1837 and written by American author Robert Montgomery Bird. The story depicts bloodshed on the frontier between Native Americans and white settlers in Kentucky. When the word "brash" is used by the character "Roaring Ralph" Stackpole, the author defines it in a footnote as meaning "rash, head-strong, over-valiant." Ralph, described in the novel as a demi-barbarian, a horse-thief, and a former Regulator, is a frontiersman based loosely on Davy Crockett, likely intended to be of Scots-Irish ancestry. Appearances of the word "brash" increase in the second half of the nineteenth century, particularly in American texts such as Mark Twain's 1884 novel *Adventures of Huckleberry Finn*.

There is a set of words of Germanic origin with similar sounds whose meanings suggest loose associations with brash, such as Old Icelandic *barr* ("vigorous"), German *brunst* ("lust; rutting season, heat") and *barsch* ("harsh, curt, abrupt"), Lowland Scots "brasche" ("violent onset, attack, assault; a fit of illness") and English "brastle" (now obsolete, "to crack; crackle; boast, brag"). These seem more like distant cousins, however, than direct ancestors.

It would be unwise to ignore the fact that the Gaelic adjective *bras*, used to describe people who are forward, boastful, or defiant, can be traced back to the early medieval period. It is used in the portrayals of warriors such as Cú Chulainn in the early Gaelic sagas. It also appears in the ninth-century wisdom text *Tecosca Cormaic* "The instructions of Cormac" which characterizes human traits and archetypes, one example being *éslessach cech brass* "every boaster is neglectful."

The adjective *bras* is amply attested in Scottish Gaelic literature of the late medieval and early modern period, although by this time it acquired the additional connotations "keen, active, energetic, brisk." In a devotional poem to the Virgin Mary composed by Maol-Domhnaigh Morrison of Mull in the early sixteenth century, a sinner is described as having a *nós bras* "haughty disposition." In an elegy for the chieftain Sir Lachlann MacLean of the MacLeans of Duart in Mull, after his death in 1649, gaming pieces are described imaginatively as *cnaip na h-àraiche braise* "cubes of boisterous battle." Hereditary poet Niall MacMhuirich described the Clanranald chieftain Domhnall mac Eòin in 1686 as *Eo Seile's am bradan bras* "The salmon of the river Seil, the brisk salmon."

A song exhorting the clans to join the 1715 Jacobite Rising begins by flattering the men of Scotland as being *bras meanmnach* "bold and high-spirited." In an erotic poem composed by the renowned Alasdair mac Mhaighstir Alasdair, in which he delights in a mistress who may or may not represent Prince Charles Edward Stuart, the adjective *bras* is used as an intensifier to describe their love-making: *bras mhacnas dian sin* "that intense, brash wantonness."

The Reverend Tormod MacLeod (1783-1862) was extremely influential in the development of a modern prose literary tradition in Gaelic, especially by editing and publishing periodicals. He composed many original texts for them himself. In a prose dialog MacLeod wrote in 1840, as socio-economic conditions were deteriorating even further in the Highlands, two fictionalized characters contemplate their future. When Para Mór tells Fionnlagh that he has made reservations for himself and his family on an emigrant ship, Fionnlagh responds, *tha eagal orm gun robh thu bras* "I'm afraid that you were impetuous."

The evidence suggests that "brash" had limited use in peripheral dialects of the anglophone world, especially in northern regions, until it took off as an American slang term in the second half of the nineteenth century. It is possible that Gaelic *bras* merged with or reinforced a similar element of Germanic origin to produce "brash" in English, but ignoring the likely Gaelic basis of the word "brash" would be ... impetuous, rash, and head-strong. It's a good thing we have a word for that.

Dour

The adjective "dour" is used of people who have a personality or countenance that is stern, grim, gloomy, sullen, or stubborn. The Scots are often stereotyped as a people who are dour by nature, so it may seem only natural that the word came into English via Lowland Scots. It appears as early as the fourteenth century in Lowland Scots literature. Blind Harry described William Wallace in an epic poem, composed in the 1480s, as being "dour in his contenance." This adjective can also refer to things that are grim and gloomy, like the weather.

"Dour" was popularized by Scottish authors such as Robert Burns and Robert Fergusson in the late eighteenth century. In Walter Scott's 1816 *The Antiquary*, the women of the family of Glenallan are described as "a doughty and a dour race." The adjective soon began to gain traction more widely in English literature in the nineteenth century. In one scene of Emily Brontë's 1847 *Wuthering Heights*, the character Heathcliff is portrayed as pacing "dumb and dour to his chamber."

Despite some claims that "dour" was borrowed into Lowland Scots from French or directly from Latin, there is a stronger case for it coming from Scottish Gaelic *dùr*. Not only does the Gaelic adjective have virtually the same set of connotations – "dull; stubborn, intractable; surly; cold, indifferent; steady, persevering, earnest" – the pronunciation matches as well, which it would not had it come into Lowland Scots from French. Had it come from Latin, we would expect to find it in medieval English as well.

The Gaelic adjective *dùr* was probably an early medieval borrowing from Latin *durus* "hard, rough; harsh; unyielding; severe," but it quickly gathered its own set of associations and usages across a range of medieval Gaelic literature. It is ironic, given the common stereotype of dour Scots, that medieval Gaels thought that it best suited the Saxons! In a poem composed sometime between the tenth and twelfth centuries listing thirteen ethnic groups and their national characteristics, we find the quip *dúre na Saxan snámach* "the dourness of the sailing Saxain."

In a poem composed by Donnchadh Campbell in the early sixteenth century in praise of Eòin MacGregor, chief of his clan, both the leader and his father Pàdraig are praised for their generosity to the men of art:

dá shaorshlait nár dhúr ré dáimh "(they are) two noble wands who are not surly (dour) to poet-bands." Slightly earlier, a poet known only as Am Bard Mac an t-Saoir, active around Rannoch and Badenoch, applied *dúr* metaphorically to the sea on which a ship was sailing: *muir dúrdha danardha* "a surly, impudent sea."

There have been plenty of opportunities for describing people and things in the modern vernacular literary tradition of "Caledonia, stern and wild" as well. In a drinking song attributed to Alasdair mac Mhaighstir Alasdair that offers toasts to the Jacobite cause and extols the transformative virtues of alcohol, the poet boasts: *Nì e brosgalach fear dùr* "It will put a dour man in a mood to flatter." When the object of his affections married another man, Uilleam Ros (1762-*c*.1791) grieved:

Ach 's truagh gum beil do rùn-sa
Cho dùr dha mo leanmhuinn ...

But it is a pity that your affections

Are so dour to my pursuit ...

In a song composed during his missionary work in the late eighteenth and early nineteenth centuries among Scottish Highland immigrants in Nova Scotia, the Reverend James MacGregor lamented the defiance of unrepentant unbelievers: *'Siad mo thruaighe clann daoine, co baoghalt, 's co dùr!* "People are the cause of my misery, so foolish and so stubborn!"

Perhaps the use of "dour" in the senses stubborn, stern and intractable is best applied to those etymologists who look exclusively to German, French, and Latin to explain obscure words in English and Lowland Scots, and pride themselves in their ignorance of Gaelic.

Jilt

The earliest examples of the verb "jilt" in modern English to mean "to reject or desert someone, most commonly a sweetheart or a suitor" survive from the 1670s. It was used in the more general sense of "deceive, trick, prove false or faithless" from the 1660s on. There are also examples between the late seventeenth and nineteenth centuries of a noun "jilt" to refer to a woman of loose morals who cannot be trusted. The word seems to have emerged first around London. The book *The London Jilt; Or, the Politick Whore* was a highly popular novel published anonymously in 1685 that depicts a young woman whose sudden family destitution forces her into prostitution.

It has been suggested that the noun "jilt" was a shortened form of Middle English "gille," a derogatory term for a young woman, or of Lowland Scots "jillet," used of a giddy or capricious girl, but these are educated guesses rather than certainties. The lexicographer and antiquarian Thomas Blount noted in the 1674 edition of his book *Glossographia*, about words in English, that jilt "is a new canting word, signifying to deceive and defeat ones expectation, more especially in the point of Amours": by his reckoning, it was slang that had not been in circulation for long.

It would be unwise to overlook the possibility that the Gaelic verb *diùlt* "refuse, deny, reject, decline, disown" contributed to the emergence of the English word, even if there may be multiple influences at play. *Diùlt* (pronounced like "joolt" in English spelling) can be found in Gaelic texts from the early medieval period onward. It was frequently used to describe rejection of the Christian message and is prominent in the medieval Gaelic commentaries about Peter's three acts of denial of Jesus in the New Testament.

Diùlt became a commonplace motif used in songs in praise of warriors in the seventeenth century, portraying them as hunters wielding guns *nach diùltadh* "that would not refuse to fire." It can also be found in Gaelic love songs, more specifically, songs about the rejection of sweethearts. In a song dated to the seventeenth century, a woman enumerates all of the high-born Highland male suitors that her friend has rejected:

Chuala mi gun d' dhiùlt thu 'n t-àrmann
Mac Fhir Bheàrnaraidh na h-Earadh.

Chuala mi gun d' dhiùlt thu 'n t-uasal
Le chruachan 's le thaighean geala.

Dhiùlt thu mac Fhir Locha Beòraich
Duine còir mac 'ille Chaluim.

Dhiùlt thu mac Fhir Locha Mhùideart
O leitir dhubhghorm an daraich.

Dhiùlt thu mac Fhionghuin a' chléirich
Le chuilbheirean geura geala.

Dhiùlt thu mac Bhàillidh Cinn Tìre
Gu cinnteach cha robh e math dhut.

Dhiùlt thu deagh Mhac 'ic Dhùbhghaill

An Caiptean a shiùbhladh tamall.

Gu dé nist a bhios tu 'g iarraidh
'S nach gabh thu iarla no baran?

I heard that you refused the stalwart
Son of the tacksman of Bernera-Harris.

I heard that you refused the noble,
With his corn stacks and his white houses.

You refused the son of Loch Beorach
The kindly man MacLeod of Raasay.

You refused young Kinlochmoidart,
From the dark-green oak-covered hillside.

You refused MacKinnon, son of the cleric,
With his bright slender guns.

You refused the son of the Chamberlain of Kintyre,
Certainly he was not good enough for you?

You refused good MacDonald of Morar,
The Captain who'd march a while.

What are you asking for now,
When you won't take an earl or a baron?

If "jilt" was brought to London in the seventeenth century from the Highlands, it was not by women of humble station but by men of high social status. King James VI of Scotland was followed by many of his fellow Scots when he began King of England and relocated to the English capital in 1603, initiating a long-standing trend. By the year 1700, there was an estimated 35,000 Scots in London, far more men than women. Although not all of them were Gaelic speakers, it is not unreasonable to expect that some were. Perhaps "jilt" started as a way for Scottish men to discuss their marital infidelities and sexual dalliances between themselves in code by adapting the Gaelic *diùlt*. This is my own conjecture, and the etymological authorities may well jilt me for it.

Glom

The English verb "glom" means "grab, snatch, seize" and is primarily associated with North American slang. It is frequently used with the preposition "onto" to mean "to become attached to" or "to become fixated on" in sentences such as "She glommed onto her purse when she saw the thief" or "Viewers have glommed onto the new television series."

"Glom" makes its earliest appearance in Jack London's autobiographical memoir *The Road*, published in 1907. It was defined as "to grab; to snatch; to take; implying violence" in a collection of criminal slang published in 1914. It seems to have entered greater circulation in the 1920s, and acquired an implication of wrongdoing. In the Disney cartoon universe, Scrooge McDuck's arch-rival is Flintheart Glomgold, depicted as a resolute and ruthless money-grabber.

The modern American "glom" is likely derived from the Lowland Scots verb "glaum," with essentially the same set of meanings and usages. It is first recorded in Lowland texts of the late eighteenth century, such as a song by Robert Burns about the Battle of Sheriffmuir, which refers to clans "wha glaum'd at kingdoms three, man." The word continued to be commonly used in Lowland Scots throughout the nineteenth and early twentieth century.

Both Lowland Scots "glaum" and American English "glom" are borrowings from Scottish Gaelic *glam*, although it is not clear whether it was loaned directly into American English from Gaelic or via Lowland Scots. The Gaelic word *glam* means "gobble, devour; seize, snatch; handle awkwardly." The Gaelic word *glòmag* "a handful of oatmeal," which exists in the dialects of Caithness, Sutherland, and Lewis, is derived from it.

An interesting example of the word *glam* occurs in an article about the interaction between Gaelic and Lowland Scots tongues published in a Gaelic journal in 1917, which states of English, *Cha do ghlam i air na facail is fheàrr a tha againn* "It did not glom onto the best words that we have."

Gaelic does indeed have a huge store of diverse, colorful, nuanced words: you should glom onto a few for yourself.

Smidge, Smidgen

The noun "smidge" or "smidgen," which is sometimes spelled "smidgeon" or "smidgin," is a slang word for a small amount of something, most common today in American English but to be found in Lowland Scots in the nineteenth century. The first recorded use of the word in English is in the 1822 novel *Sir Andrew Wylie* by Ayrshire native John Galt: "I ken vera weel that ye dinna like to hae sic a wee smytch o' apartner as me." A poem written in 1836 by John Ramsay of Kilmarnock, another Ayrshire native, has "But every smitch o't was a kin' o' red."

The word began to appear widely in the United States by the late nineteenth century, written most often as "smitch." The spelling "smidge" did not gain currency until the early twentieth century.

Scholars have suggested that "smidge" is related to the verb "smite," so that it would imply a fragment struck off of something. This may well explain some of the senses of the word, but the Gaelic *smid* must have contributed significantly to its pedigree as well. The Gaelic noun *smid* means "a sound, syllable, word" and is generally used to emphasize assertions in the negative, such as *Cha tuirt e smid* "He didn't say a single thing." *Smid* is pronounced exactly the same as "smidge" in English.

The earliest surviving example of *smid* in a Gaelic text occurs in Scottish context: the celebrated poem "Soraidh slán don oidhche a-rér" by the master poet Niall Mór MacMhuirich, who was active in the late sixteenth and early seventeenth centuries. On first reading, the poem seems to be about a secret love affair between the poet and a woman he sees at a gathering in a chieftain's hall, although there are many layers to the text and ways of interpreting it. The stanza in which *smid* appears is this:

Nocha leigid luchd nam breug
smid as mo bhéal, a rosg mall:
tuig an ní adeir mo shúil
agus tú san chúil úd thall.

The folk of lies do not allow
one peep from my lip, o languid eye:
understand the thing my eye says,

though you are in yonder corner.

Smid can be found widely in Scottish Gaelic texts from the seventeenth century onward. One of the reasons to suspect that "smidgen" and its variations are Gaelic loanwords is the ending: one of the ways to create a diminutive form of a noun in Gaelic is to append -*ean* or -*an* to it, which would explain why we find both "smidge" and "smidgen" in English with the same meaning. The pronunciation of this reconstructed diminutive form *smidean* is exactly the same - with the same syllabic emphasis - as the English "smidgeon."

This claim to Scottish Gaelic origin would make "smidge" and "smidgen" cousins to the word "smithereen," which was borrowed from Irish into English. The original Irish word *smidirín* is based on the same root as Scottish Gaelic *smid* and conveys the same meaning.

There are enough Gaelic loanwords in English that when someone asks you if you speak Gaelic, you can always truthfully answer, "Just a smidge."

Spunk

The noun "spunk" is used commonly in modern English to refer to courage, pluckiness, mettle, vivacity, and vital spark. These are mostly metaphorical extensions of its earlier meaning, "kindling, firewood, spark." It is also a slang term for semen. "Spunk" is the title of a short story written by Zora Neale Hurston, and the nickname of its main character. It was also used as the name of albums by the Sex Pistols and the Swamp Zombies.

"Spunk" can be found in Lowland Scots texts as early as the sixteenth century with the meaning "a spark of fire" and in the seventeenth century to refer to matchsticks for lighting fires. The poem "The Ordination" that Robert Burns wrote and published in 1786 uses it in this literal sense: "We'll light a spunk ..." Slightly earlier, in 1777, the Lowland Scots poet Robert Fergusson used it in a metaphorical sense for the spark of existence: "Life's Spunk decay'd, nae mair can blaze."

This word is an early borrowing from Scottish Gaelic into Lowland Scots referring specifically to tinder, firewood, and timber fuel. The traditional Gaelic idiom *cho tioram ri spuing* "as dry as tinder" attests to this usage.

Hewing wood and making matchsticks was one of many things that men did as they listened to folktales and songs during the *céilidh*s held on long winter evenings, as recalled in this sketch from the later nineteenth century:

> The mode of producing light was by striking a spark from a piece of flint or quartz, which spark falling on a piece of charred linen or cotton, set it on fire, and this again was made use of to light a rude match made of fir and tipped with brimstone.

> The making of these matches, or "spunks" as they were called, gave occupation in the long evenings to the male part of the family, who split up fine pieces of fir, and dipped the ends into melted brimstone or sulphur, and thus produced a rude lucifer match.

Before artificial chemicals such as these were available, Highland shepherds collected fungus growing in trees - called *spong* or *spuing* in Gaelic - for use as fire starters. The previous entry about the word BELTANE mentions the use of fungus for lighting the ritual bonfire: "So soon as any sparks were emitted by means of the violent friction, they applied a species of agaric which grows on old birch-trees, and is very combustible." This material takes us back to the origin of the term in Gaelic as a medieval borrowing of Latin *spongia* "a sponge."

Bore

One of the senses of the verb "bore" is to create a feeling of weariness, tediousness, impatience, or dullness in someone, especially by talking about a subject in which the listener has no interest. "Bore" began to appear in the English of England in this sense in the second half of the eighteenth century but became more common in the nineteenth century.

The standard explanation of this slang usage is the analogy that dull and tedious conversation is like boring, or drilling, through the ears to the brain, but influence from Gaelic is also likely. The verb *bodhair* means in a literal sense "to deafen or stun with noise," and is pronounced nearly the same as "bore" in English. The Gaelic verb can also used to express the displeasure or tedium of listening to someone talking.

Sìleas na Ceapaich MacDonald composed a song in the early eighteenth century expressing her disapproval of loose sexual mores and her concern of their effects on her daughters. Her long condemnation of debauchery begins:

> *'S mise th' air mo bhodhradh*
> *Le toghnadh na h-oba nodha,*
> *Ag éisteachd nan daoine*
> *A' laoidh mar nì iad an gnothach ...*

> I am deafened / bothered
> By the noise of the new charms,
> Listening to people
> Discussing how they "do the business" ...

Another typical example occurs in one of the dialog texts printed in the 1840s meant to acquaint Highlanders with the world of anglophone modernity, often relying on characters that personified particular qualities, cultural affinities or political stances:

> *Stad thusa gus am faic mise Lachann nan Ceistean; tha mi air mo bhodhradh leis; cha chluinnear aige ach am fasan Gallda, biodh daoine beo no marbh; ach ma tha e 'n dàn dhomhs' 'fhaicinn, cuiridh mi 'ghlas-ghuib air an déidh na chunnaic mi 'n-diugh.*

> Wait until I see Lachann the Catechist; I am bored by him; you don't hear about anything from him but alien fashions, regardless of whether people

are living or dead; but if I am fated to see him, I'll muzzle him after what I saw today.

The conjecture that Scottish Gaelic *bodhair* was borrowed into English as "bore," or at least influenced this usage, is supported by the parallel borrowing of the same Gaelic word into English as "bother." The verb was used in medieval Gaelic texts to convey the senses of "confuse, trouble, perturb" as well "deafen," and it is unclear as to whether "bother" came into English from Irish or Scottish Gaelic, or from both independently.

The nineteenth-century Irish scholar Patrick Joyce left a valuable discussion of the relationship between these words in anglophone and Gaelic-speaking communities in Ireland:

> It appears to me obvious that bother is merely the Irish *bodhar*, deaf, although I know very well that a different origin has been assigned to it. For, first, it is in universal use - it is literally in every one's mouth - in Ireland. Secondly, what is more to the purpose, while it is used, as it is in England, to signify annoyance or trouble, it has another meaning in Ireland which is not known in England, namely, deaf, the same as the original word *bodhar*; and this is obviously its primary meaning. A person who is either partly or wholly deaf is said to be bothered; and this usage is perfectly familiar in every part of Ireland, from Dublin to the remotest districts - among the educated as well as among the illiterate. The word indeed in this sense, is the foundation of a proverb :- you are said to "turn the bothered ear" to a person when you do not wish to hear what he says, or grant his request. Moreover, so well are the two words bother and *bodhar* understood to be identical, that in the colloquial language of the peasantry they are always used to translate each other.

One of the dangers of becoming passionate about Gaelic is the likelihood of either boring or bothering monoglot anglophones with the unappreciated beauties and hidden histories of the language. These are tendencies covered by one word, *bodhair*, in Gaelic and two in English!

Dig, Twig

"Can you dig it?" Anyone who lived through the 1970s should remember that phrase from anglophone popular culture. The verb "dig" in this usage, meaning "to understand; to like," has been said to date back to the 1930s in African-American slang, although corroborating contemporary examples are not easily found.

It is much easier to detect it in the popular culture of the late 1960s and '70s. The African-American band Friends of Distinction, formed in Los Angeles, released the song "Grazing in the Grass" in 1968. The chorus includes the words "I can dig it, he can dig it, She can dig it, we can dig it ..." The Beatles released their album *Let It Be* in May 1970 which includes a song called "Dig It." The phrase quickly entered mainstream usage.

There are three main theories about the origins of this idiom in North America. One is that it is simply an extension of the English verb "dig" in the sense of "to excavate," acquiring the sense "to reveal through effort." Another theory is that it is derived from the word *dëgg, dëgga* "to understand, appreciate" in the Wolof language of Africa. A third theory is that it derived from the Irish verb *tuig* "to understand, perceive," which, when used in context, is usually pronounced very similarly to English "dig."

It seems very likely that the American slang term "dig" is related in some way to the verb "twig" in the slang of England. "Twig" emerges in textual sources in the second half of the eighteenth century and becomes more common in the nineteenth century. Its meaning and usage – "to realize, notice" – is very similar to "dig." This word in the English of England is almost certainly a borrowing of the Gaelic verb *tuig* meaning "to understand, perceive, discern, comprehend." Although the same verb exists in Irish, its pronunciation in Scottish Gaelic matches the loan in English better than the Irish form.

As we have seen frequently in these word histories, it is often the case that slang terms do not necessarily have a single exclusive origin but result from the convergence of words that sound similar and have similar meanings as communities co-mingle and interact with one another, sharing space, words, and culture. The Gaelic speakers of both Scotland and Ireland brought *tuig* with them as basic vocabulary when they emigrated to North America, and it is not difficult to imagine how American "dig" could have emerged as the intersection of usage in encounters with the British slang "twig" and Wolof *dëgg*.

This word, in fact, serves to illustrate how much English is a mongrel language, a hybrid formed by the encounters of many different peoples. Tracing the words that have come into common usage brings us into contact with a multitude of stories and ethnic groups that reach far beyond the simplistic stereotypes of Anglo-Saxons and British monarchs. While Scottish Gaels are just one among many who have made contributions to the evolution of English, their stories also deserve to be recognized and understood - to be twigged.

Appendix: A Chronological Analysis

The chart below displays the borrowings from Scottish Gaelic into various forms of English from the fourteenth to the twentieth century, indicating whether the borrowing happened in Scotland (marked with "S"), in England (marked with "E"), or North America (marked with "NA").

This chart highlights common patterns in these cross-cultural exchanges. It is immediately obvious that during the first four centuries nearly all borrowings are within Scotland itself across the Highland-Lowland divide. Most of the words in play relate to portable physical objects, features of the landscape, or social roles and practices that would have been visible to, and impactful on, anglophones in the Scottish Lowlands. There are no verbs or abstract nouns, and only one adjective, in the early borrowings.

It is not until the later eighteenth century, when anglophones and Gaels came into much greater contact with one another through emigration, travel, military conflict, and the literary imagination, that the range of types of borrowings expands to include verbs, adjectives, and more subtle forms of culture.

It is also noteworthy that the majority of more recent borrowings have happened in North American contexts. This is not surprising given the large-scale emigration of Gaelic speakers from the Highlands into nearly every corner of North America, with the language sometimes lasting for several generations and influencing adjacent communities.

	14	15	16	17	18	19	20
Cateran	S						
Crag	S						
Dour	S						
Bard		S					
Beltane		S					
Loch		S					
Clan			S	E			

	14	15	16	17	18	19	20
Slogan			S			E	
Cairn			S				
Coronach			S				
Blackmail			S		E		
Galloglass			E				
Pillion			S				
Scone			S				
Pet			S				
Caber			S				
Ingle			S				
Bog			S				
Ptarmigan			S				
Gob			S				
Spunk			S				
Gillie				S			
Whisky				S			
Trews, Trousers				S			
Dulse				S			
Galore				E			
Jilt				E			
Sassenach					S		
Banshee					E		
Claymore					S		
Spree					S		
Strathspey					S		
Croon					S		

	14	15	16	17	18	19	20
Bothy					E		
Cosy, Cozy					S		
Glaum					S		
Bore					E		
Twig					E		
Fore						S	
Shindig						NA	
Brash						E	
Smidge(n)						S	
Mac							NA
Oscar							NA
Boogie							NA
Grotty							E
Grody							NA
Snazzy							NA
Glom							NA
Dig							NA

Notes and Sources

Introduction: What is Language?

The quote from Robert McDougall interpreting words from First Nation languages as though they were in Gaelic is from McDougall, *Ceann-Iùil an Fhir-Imrich*, 38, 41, 44, 48.

The quote by Mackay is from *The Gaelic Etymology*, xix, xxxii.

The criticism about Daniel Cassidy is from Barrett, "Humdinger."

The explanation of the origins of the word "shanty" is from Hutson, "Gaelic Loan-Words," 19.

Introduction: Wars of Words

The history of the development of literacy and literature in Gaelic is explored in Ó Cróinín, *Early Medieval Ireland*, 186-89, 196-232 and Ó Cathasaigh, "The literature of medieval Ireland to c.800."

The background to *Sanas Cormaic* (*Cormac's Glossary*) can be found in Stifter, "Old Irish Etymologies."

Discussion of the manuscript containing a glossary of Gaelic words in verse form can be found in Ó Maolalaigh, "DASG," 251.

The poetry by Robert Campbell of Cowall is from Evans and Roberts, *Edward Lhwyd*, 88-89. The ode by the Reverend John MacLean can be found in McLeod and Newton, *An Ubhal as Àirde*, 184, 185.

Information about the life of Alasdair mac Mhaighstir Alasdair is from Thomson, *Alasdair mac Mhaighstir Alasdair*, 1-3, 135-37. The Gaelic verses quoted by him are from pages 77-78 of the same source, the translation into English is mine.

Information about Alasdair mac Mhaighstir Alasdair's vocabulary is from Thomson, *Alasdair mac Mhaighstir Alasdair*, 17-19. Meek, "The Gaelic Literary Enlightenment," discusses Dugald Buchanan's petition to create a dictionary. Details about early Scottish Gaelic dictionaries is from Thomson, *The Companion to Gaelic Scotland*, 61-62, 67-68.

Discussion about scholarship investigating the influence of Gaelic on English can be found in Thier, "Of Picts and Penguins," 246-47.

The quote from William Mackay is from Mackay, "Celtic Words," 327.

Information about *DASG* can be found in Ó Maolalaigh, "DASG." The history of *Am Faclair Beag* was communicated to me personally by Michael Bauer.

Introduction: Language Contact and Exchange

I have taken the summary of the derivation of "curse" from Liberman, "Blessing and cursing, part 3: curse (conclusion)." A summary of the history of the influence of the Columban church on Northumbria can be found in Grimmer, "Columban Christian Influence," 99-103, 106-09.

The distribution of Gaelic and Lowland Scots tongues in Scotland at the beginning of the eighteenth century is discussed in Pons-Sanz and MacCoinnich, "The Languages of Scotland," 19.

The quote by Lachann MacBheathain is from MacBheathain, "Buaidh na Gàidhlig," 19. My translation.

A summary of the history of the scholarship about Lowland Scots can be found on the webpage "History of Scots to 1700" in the online *Dictionary of the Scots Language* at https://dsl.ac.uk/about-scots/history-of-scots/vocabulary/

For information about Gaelic loanwords in Lowland Scots, see the respective entries for the words mentioned in the *Dictionary of the Scots Language* as well as Breeze, "Gaelic Vocabulary," 225-26. Legal terminology borrowed from Gaelic into Lowland Scots is discussed in Barrow, "The lost Gàidhealtachd," 73-74.

The quote about Gaelic-speaking African-Americans is cited and discussed in Newton, "'Did You Hear About The Gaelic-Speaking African?'," 91. The quote from the Scottish minister about Gaelic-speaking First Nations peoples in the North-West Territory of Canada is from *The Scottish-American Journal* 6 April 1902.

Information about the writings of Walter Scott as a conduit of Gaelic borrowings can be found in Dossena, " 'Sassenach', eh?," 69-70.

The final quote is from MacBheathain, "Buaidh na Gàidhlig," 31-32. My translation.

Scot

The earliest surviving usages of the ethnonym "Scot(ti)" are discussed in Koch, *Celtic Culture*, 1572. The proposed derivation of this term from Gaelic is discussed in McCone, *The Celtic Question*, 12. The poem by Gofraidh Fionn Ó Dálaigh has been edited in Knott, "Filidh Éireann," 60-61.

A discussion of origin legends including Scota daughter of Pharaoh can be found in Ó Riain, "The Metz Version," 42-44. A useful and up-to-date summary of relations between the dynasties of Pictland and Dál Riata can be found in Foster, *Picts, Gaels and Scots*, 35-36 and Woolf, *From Pictland to Alba*, 60-67.

The development and meaning of the terms "Scot" and "Scotland" is discussed in Woolf, "Reporting Scotland," 227-28 and Woolf, "The 'When, Why

& Wherefore' of Scotland," 14. The medieval transformation of the usage of the term "Scot" is discussed in MacGregor, "Gaelic Barbarity," 37-43.

Sassenach

The Gaelic understanding of the words *Sasannach* and *Gall* as explained by John MacInnes can be found in MacInnes, *Dùthchas nan Gàidheal*, 38. Further discussion of this terminology and the problems that modern scholars have had understanding it can be found in McLeod, "Gaelic Poetry," 174-77.

Patrick Graham's account of the place names in Aberfoyle can be found in Graham, *Sketches of Perthshire*, 183-84.

Discussion of the ethnonym *Sasannach* in Scottish place names can be found in Morgan, *Ethnonyms in the Place-names*, 114. The usage and development of ethnonyms based on *Gall* is discussed in McLeod, *Divided Gaels*, 20-33, 126-30.

The quote by James MacKenzie is found in MacKenzie, *History of Scotland*, 608. Discussion of Lowland Scots identifying as Teutons and Anglo-Saxons can be found in Kidd, "Teutonic Ethnology."

The verses by Màiri Mhór nan Òran can be found in Meek, *Màiri Mhòr*, 108. My translation. The dialog quoted comes from Kidd, *Còmhraidhean nan Cnoc*, 110. My translation. The quote from the Gaelic history book is from MacChoinnich, *Bliadhna Thearlaich*, 128. My translation.

Mac

The quote about the unreliability of Highland surnames is from Matheson, *Highland Surnames*, 3, 6.

Discussion of the usage of "mac" as slang can be found in *Oxford English Dictionary*, "Mac." The article is Safire, "On Language." The quote about the surname MacRath / MacRae / etc is from MacPhail, *Highland Papers*, vol. 1, 198.

Further discussion about how Gaelic surnames have been anglicized, distorted and mangled can be found in Black, *The Surnames of Scotland*, xl-xli.

Oscar

Some background history about how the Oscars got their name can be found in Hiskey, "Why are the Academy Awards Statues Called Oscars?"

The history of the character Oscar / Osgar, as well as the role of the Fian as a whole, in Gaelic tradition is discussed in MacKillop, *Oxford Dictionary of Celtic Mythology*, 358 and Newton, *Warriors of the Word*, 335, 337.

Clan

For the history of the word "clan" in English, see *Oxford English Dictionary*, "clan," and *Dictionary of the Scots Language*, "clan." For the history of the word in Gaelic, and other words for kin-groups, see Koch, *Celtic Culture*, 452-53 and Bannerman, "The Scots Language," 5-6.

For details about the way that Highland clans were named, structured and functioned, see Newton, *The Everyday Life of the Clans*, 74-92. For discussion of the clan names in the Book of Deer, see Sellar, "The Family," 93.

For discussion of the origin of the KKK and intersections with Highlandism, see Newton, "The History of the Fiery Cross," 38-39.

Slogan

For the history of the word "slogan" in English, see the *Oxford English Dictionary*, "slogan."

The quote about the Buchanans is adapted from Buchanan, *Account of the Family of Buchanan*, 165-66.

Cairn

For the history of the word "cairn" in English, see the *Oxford English Dictionary*, "cairn."

The origin of the name "Cairngorms" is discussed in Alexander, *The Cairngorms*, 21.

The excerpt from *Togail bruidne Dá Derga* is taken from Koch, *The Celtic Heroic Age*, 179. The quote from the anonymous Highland source from c.1685 can be found in Campbell, *A Collection of Highland Rites*, 43. The quote from Martin Martin can be found in Martin, *A description of the Western Isles*, 151-52. The quote from Edmund Burt can be found in Simmons, *Burt's Letters*, 244-45.

The deep history of the word *carn* in Celtic languages is discussed in Koch, "Ériu, Alba, and Letha," 24.

Bard

The quotes from ancient texts can be found in Koch, *The Celtic Heroic Age*, 13, 14, and 11. For details about the professional poetic orders and their shifting social status, see Newton, *Warriors of the Word*, 89-91, 97-101.

The quote from the history of the Campbells of Craignish can be found in Campbell, "The Manuscript History," 190. For the medieval notices about bards in Lowland Scotland, see *Dictionary of the Scots Language*, "bard."

Gillie, Ghillie

For the history of the word "gillie" in Lowland Scots, see *Dictionary of the Scots Language*, "gillie."

The Scottish Country Sports Tourism Group webpage quoted is at https://countrysportscotland.com/other-info/stalkers-ghillies-and-keepers/

The dance Gille Chaluim is discussed in Flett and Flett, *Traditional Step-Dancing in Scotland*, 25-28. References to the use of soft shoes called "ghillies" can be found in *Dictionary of the Scots Language*, "gillie."

The early meanings and uses of the term *gilla* can be inferred from *Electronic Dictionary of the Irish Language*, "gilla." Explanation of the use of the term *gille* in surnames can be found in Watson, "Personal Names," 226-27 and Hammond, "Introduction," 7-8.

The terms for Highland servants can be found in Simmons, *Burt's Letters*, 220. I have corrected the Gaelic orthography and provided more accurate translations than the original source.

Coronach

The quote from Edmund can be found in Simmons, *Burt's Letters*, 244.

The Gaelic song upon which Scott's "Coronach" is based is generally referred to by its first line "Tha mo shealgair 'na shìneadh."

Alexander Scott's poem "Coronach" has been recently reprinted in the anthology edited by Goldie and Watson, *From the Line*, 167-68.

For a discussion of keening in Gaelic society, see Newton, *Warriors of the Word*, 183-85.

For the satirical poem about bagpipes, see McLeod and Bateman, *Duanaire na Sracaire*, 280-81. For discussion about this poem and how it relates to the history of the bagpipes in Gaelic society, see Newton and Cheape, "'The Keening of Women'," 79-80.

Beltane

For the history of the word "Beltane" in English and Lowland Scots, see the *Oxford English Dictionary*, "beltane" and *Dictionary of the Scots Language*, "beltane."

For discussion of the term "Beltancu," and the related history of ethnic groups in Lancashire, see Breeze, "Irish 'Beltaine' May Day."

Discussion of the derivation and original meaning of the word *Bealtainn* in Gaelic can be found in Black, *The Gaelic Otherworld*, 592, Muhr, "Beltaine in Irish and Scottish Place-names," 97-100, and Koch, *Celtic Culture*, 202.

The quote from John Ramsay can be found in Allerdyce, *Scotland and Scotsmen*, vol. 2, 439-444.

Discussion of the place name Tullybelton and historical documentation about rituals there can be found in Muhr, "Beltaine in Irish and Scottish Place-names," 113-14.

Banshee

For the history of the word "banshee" in Lowland Scots, see *Dictionary of the Scots Language*, "banshee."

For the history of the *sìdhichean* / fairies in Gaelic cosmology, see Newton, *Warriors of the Word*, 221, 233-37. For discussion of the archetype of the female goddess and the connection to keening, see Ó Crualaoich, *The Book of the Cailleach*, 30-78 and Newton, *Warriors of the Word*, 157-63, 183, 203-221.

Claymore

The quote describing the Highland soldiers in 1715 is from Anon, *The Loch Lomond Expedition*, 8.

One example of the use of "claymore" in the war-cry of the Jacobites can be found in Smibert, *The Clans of the Highlands of Scotland*, 289. Many thanks to Christopher Thompson for alerting me to this material. *Dictionary of the Scots Language* also cites an occurrence in the *Scots Magazine* in 1749.

For other early examples of "claymore" in anglophone texts, see *Oxford English Dictionary*, "claymore, n."

For information about the swords imported from Germany and Spain, and Lowland imitations, see Grant and Cheape, *Periods in Highland History*, 196-97. The mid-seventeenth century poem to Lachlann MacLean can be found in Ó Baoill, *Bàrdachd Chloinn Ghill-Eathain*, 28. The elegy to Alasdair mac Colla can be found in MacKenzie, *Òrain Iain Luim*, 34, 249. The song rallying Highlanders to join Prince Charles in 1745 can be found in Campbell, *Highland Songs*, 128.

The complex literary history of Excalibur is discussed in Koch, *Celtic Culture*, 328-29.

Spree

The poem by William Lillie is quoted and discussed by Sayers, "Two Etymologies," 47. Sayers suggested that "spree" is derived from Gaelic *spraic* "reprimand, frown, command, vigor, exertion, sprightliness, cleverness" but this seems less likely to me than the derivation I propose.

Electronic Dictionary of the Irish Language documents the historical usage of the word *spréidh*, for example, in the tale "Aislinge Meic Conglinne," which is dated to the late eleventh or early twelfth century.

The excerpt from the poem attributed to Rachel MacGregor can be found in McLeod and Newton, *An Ubhal as Àirde*, 389, 390.

The borrowing of Gaelic *spréidh* into Lowland Scots is discussed in *Dictionary of the Scots Language*, "spreth" and Pödör, "Scottish Gaelic Loanwords," 181.

The quote from Pennant can be found in Pennant, *A Tour In Scotland. 1769*, 176-77.

The history and usages of the word *spréd* can be gleaned from *Electronic Dictionary of the Irish Language*, "spréidid." O'Rahilly's discussion is in "Etymological Notes," 65.

Blackmail

The history of the word "blackmail" can be found in *Oxford English Dictionary*, "blackmail." I have modernized the spelling of the Scottish Act of 1567.

The customs and practices regarding cattle-raiding in Gaeldom are discussed in detail in Lucas, *Cattle in Ancient Ireland*, 125-99. Further aspects of these practices in a Scottish context are discussed in Macinnes, *Clanship*, 32-37 and Newton, *Warriors of the Word*, 134.

The quote from Martin Martin can be found in his *A Description of the Western Isles*, 101-02.

For discussion of blackmail as a sign of disruption and destabilization in Highland society, see Grant and Cheape, *Periods in Highland History*, 151-71, Macinnes, *Clanship*, 46-52, and Newton, *Warriors of the Word*, 26-27.

The quote from Loch Lomond-side is from Dewar, *The Dewar Manuscripts*, 92-93.

Discussion of the borrowing *màl* into Gaelic and the practice of paying tribute can be found in Grant and Cheape, *Periods in Highland History*, 147 and *Electronic Dictionary of the Irish Language*, "mál."

The idea that *dubh* refers to the color of cattle is offered in Ghriogair, *Ri Luinneig*, 52. Thanks to Àdhamh Ó Broin for the suggestion that it may refer to something hidden or obscure. The word *dubh* appears in two different terms in Irish that describe parallel protection payments: "dowgollo," an anglicized form, and *duibhchíos*. See Simms, *Kings and Warlords*, 144-45.

Cateran

The history of the word "cateran" in Lowland Scots and English is discussed in *Oxford English Dictionary*, "cateran" and Pödör, "Scottish Gaelic Loanwords," 177. Dunbar's poem is "Sir Thomas Norny."

For the history and associations of the word *ceatharn* in Gaelic, see Simms, "Gaelic warfare in the Middle Ages," 100. The quote from the history of the Campbells of Craignish is from Campbell, "The Manuscript History," 201.

The quote about "broken men" and blackmail is from Macinnes, *Clanship, Commerce and the House of Stuart*, 32.

The quote from the mid-eighteenth-century Highland antiquarian can be found in Macpherson, *Critical Dissertations*, 129. The 1848 description of a shinty game is in MacLeod, *Caraid nan Gàidheal*, 401.

Galloglass

The history of the word "galloglass" in English is discussed in *Oxford English Dictionary*, "galloglas." The history of the galloglass and their role in Gaelic military strategy is discussed in McLeod, *Divided Gaels*, 43-44 and Duffy, "The Prehistory," 1-3.

The excerpt from Shakespeare's *Macbeth* is from Act 1, Scene 2.

The Gaelic name for lemon balm was highlighted in a tweet from @eDIL_Dictionary, the group behind *Electronic Dictionary of the Irish Language*, on November 4, 2020: https://twitter.com/eDIL_Dictionary/status/1324031628390371329

Strathspey

There is a great deal of discussion about the history of the strathspey in the eighteenth century and perceptions of it in contemporary Europe in Lamb, "Reeling in the Strathspey."

The long quote by Reverend Dr. William Thomson can be found in Newte, *Prospects and Observations*, 163-65. The arrival of the Baroque violin in Scotland is discussed in Alburger, "The Fiddle," 246-48. For information about the development of social dances that evolved in the Highlands in response to the importation of the fiddle and its music, see Newton, "'Dannsair air Ùrlar-Déile Thu'," 51-52, 59, 67.

Information about the history of the Cummings of Freuchie was communicated to me personally by Keith Sanger. The frequency of dotted rhythms in Gaelic, Scots, and English folk songs is discussed in Lamb, "Reeling in the Strathspey," 75-84. The incident about Prince Charles singing a strathspey is recorded in Forbes, *The Lyon in Mourning*, vol. 1, fol. 359, 191.

The question of the date of fiddle tunes containing Scotch snaps with "strathspey" in their title is discussed in Alburger, *Scottish Fiddlers*, 45-46. The concluding quote is from William Honeyman and can be found in Lamb, "Reeling in the Strathspey," 66.

Croon

The history of the word "croon" in Lowland Scots is discussed in *Dictionary of the Scots Language*, "croon." The derivation from Middle Dutch in Middle English is discussed in https://en.wiktionary.org/wiki/cronen#Middle_English

The tenth-century Gaelic poem in which *crónán* appears can be found in Carney, *Medieval Irish Lyrics*, 70. Its occurrence and meaning in medieval

Gaelic texts can be gleaned from *Electronic Dictionary of the Irish Language,* "crónán." The early texts in which *crónán* appears include strata of "Amra Choluimb Chille," "Serglige Conculaind," "Auraicept na n-éces," and "Buile Suibhne."

The legal tracts mentioned are discussed in Kelly, *Early Irish Farming,* 122. The earliest Scottish Gaelic texts in which the word can be found are given in McLeod and Newton, *An Ubhal as Àirde,* 134 and 167. The poem by Iain Lom MacDonald can be found in MacKenzie, *Òrain Iain Luim,* lines 277-79.

The anecdote about Màiri nighean Alasdair Ruaidh can be found in Ó Baoill, *Màiri nighean Alasdair Ruaidh,* 8-9. The proverb about cats can be found in Nicolson, *Gaelic Proverbs,* 239.

Boogie

For discussion of the word "boogie" and the complexities in tracking its origin, see Liberman, "Multifarious devils, part 1: 'bogey'." For the meanings and usages of the Gaelic words *bog* and *bogadh,* see *Am Faclair Beag,* "bogadh."

An edition and translation of the Gaelic song-poem composed in about 1732 can be found in Black, "Appendix 3," 141. I have altered the translation of the first line, which contains *bogadh,* to follow the individual word meanings more closely.

For a discussion of the censuring of Gaelic texts since the eighteenth century, see Campbell, *A Very Civil People,* 174-86 and Newton, *The Naughty Little Book,* xi-xii, 34, 49. For a discussion of the usage of *bogadh* to refer to sexual intercourse, see Black, *An Lasair,* 372.

The stanza from the song by George MacKenzie is from Black, *An Lasair,* 18-19. I have modified the translation slightly. The stanza from the song by Sìleas na Ceapaich is from Black, *An Lasair,* 24-25. I have modified the translation slightly, especially to highlight my understanding of *boga-bhriseadh,* literally "breaking-bobbing," as a female's first experience of sexual intercourse.

Fore

For discussion of the history of the word "fore" in Lowland Scots, see *Dictionary of the Scots Language,* "fore." I believe that I first learned of the derivation of "fore" from Gaelic from Raghnall MacGilleDhuibh while I was a student at the University of Edinburgh.

It might be argued that "fore" could not be derived from the Gaelic word *faire* because of the short vowel of the last. Once borrowed into English, however, the function of the word as an exclamation to call attention to danger would have made the original vowel length irrelevant.

Evidence that anglophones were aware of the Gaelic exclamation is discussed in Breeze, "Scots Fary," 54-55. The song by Rob Dunn is given in Campbell, *Highland Songs*, 236. The text in the novel mentioned is MacDhonnchaidh, *An t-Ogha Mór*, 211.

The use of *faire-faire!* in a song to the MacKenzies can be found in Black, *An Lasair*, 118. The bagpipe song about Cameron of Lochiall can be found in *An Gàidheal* 4 (1875): 19. The lullaby for the MacLeods of Dunvegan can be found in several variants, including "Tàladh na Mna Sìthe," in MacDougall and Calder, *Folk Tales*, 104 and Carmichael, *Ortha nan Gàidheal* vol. 5, 218. The song by Ruaidhri MacMhuirich can be found in Matheson, *An Clàrsair Dall*, 66, 68, 135.

The Gaelic influence in and on the texts of Alexander Montgomerie is discussed in Meek, "Gàidhlig agus Gaylick," 137-38, 145. The other appearance of the phrase "firy fary" can be found in *Dictionary of the Scots Language*, "wary."

For discussion of the history and meanings of the word "fary" in Lowland Scots, see *Dictionary of the Scots Language*, "fary" and Breeze, "Scots Fary," 53-54.

The quote from Gerald of Wales is given and discussed in Simms, "Images of Warfare," 615.

Shindig

The 1848 quote from Charles A. Hentz can be found in Housewright, *A History of Music and Dance in Florida*, 192. The quote from 1864 can be found in Epstein, *Sinful Tunes and Spirituals*, 141. Thanks to Phil Jamison for these two references.

The origin and historical usage of the words "shindig" and "shindy" can be found in *Oxford English Dictionary*, "shindig" and "shindy."

Details about the history of shinty in Scottish history can be found in the work of Hugh Dan MacLennan. These particular facts come from MacLennan, "Shinty's Place and Space in the World," 3. See also *Dictionary of the Scots Language*, "shinty." The quote from a Highland newspaper in 1870 can be found in MacLennan, "Shinty's Place and Space in the World," 5.

Discussion of the relationship between "shinty" and Gaelic *sìnteag* can be found in MacDonald, "Shinty," 27-28 and MacLennan, "Shinty's Place and Space in the World," 5. It is worth noting that the *-ag* ending in Gaelic signifies a diminutive, just as "-y" does in English.

The excerpt from Duncan Bàn can be found in MacLeod, *Òrain Dhonnchaidh Bhàin*, 208-09. The excerpt from *port-à-beul* about dancing can be found in Lamb, *Keith Norman MacDonald's Puirt-à-Beul*, 86.

Pillion

For the history of the word "pillion" in Lowland Scots, and the entries about Queen Margaret Tudor, see *Dictionary of the Scots Language*, "pilȝan; pillion."

The quatrain from the Gaelic satire can be found in Black, *An Lasair*, 82-83. The quatrain by Iain Lom MacDonald can be found in Macleod and Newton, *An Ubhal as Àirde*, 222, 224. I have adapted the translation. The stanza from the Skye bard can be found in MacLeòid, *Òrain Nuadh Ghaeleach*, 100. My translation.

Whisky

The earliest mention of whisky in a Gaelic context is discussed in Simms, "Guesting and Feasting," 88. The history of the word in Lowland Scots, including spelling, is discussed in *Dictionary of the Scots Language*, "Iskie-bae."

The stanza describing whisky as a Lowland drink is quoted and discussed in MacInnes, *Dùthchas nan Gàidheal*, 41. The description of the banqueting hall of Fraser of Lovat is adapted from Macleod, *Memoirs of the life and gallant exploits*, 47-48.

The advice about the effects of one to three drams of whisky is taken from Newton, *Naughty Little Book*, 25.

Trews, Trousers

The history of the word "trews" in Lowland Scots is discussed in *Dictionary of the Scots Language*, "trew(i)s."

Discussion of records about the making of trews and its place in the clothing habits of the Highland élite can be found in Cheape, "Gheibhte Breacain Chàrnaid," 26-29. The couplet describing the clothing of earl of Argyll in the sixteenth century is from McLeod and Newton, *An Ubhal as Àirde*, 117, 124. I have adapted the translation.

The idioms that refer to trousers are from Nicholson, *Gaelic Proverbs*, 160, 256, 348 and *Am Faclair Beag*, "triubhas."

Discussion about the dance *Seann Triubhas* can be found in Melin, *A Story to Every Dance*, 23-34.

Scone

The description of a scone is from *Oxford English Dictionary*, "scone." Early references to, and explanations of the usage of, the word "scone" can be found in *Dictionary of the Scots Language*, "scone."

A discussion of the standard derivation of "scone," and why it is unsatisfactory, can be found in Sayers, "Scones," 447. The meaning and usage of *sgonn* in Gaelic can be found in *Am Faclair Beag*, "sgonn" and MacMillan, *Sporan Dhomhnaill*, 413.

Ian Clayton has cautioned me that "recipient languages are prone to make all kinds of unpredictable alterations to loans. The morphological structure of the original word typically plays no role, especially if that structure isn't transparent to the borrowing language's speakers" (personal communication). The language and ethnic makeup of the specific Lowland communities where the loan happened would thus be crucial to know. Flemish-speaking immigrants settled in the Lowlands between the twelfth and sixteenth centuries and their presence is marked by a clutch of Flemish loans in Lowland Scots. "Scone" is one of those loanwords claimed in a discussion in French, "The Flemish Influence on Scottish Language." If Flemish speakers themselves were using the word in the Lowlands for a bread they were making in the region, and their language was already related to the form of English spoken in the burghs, it seems unlikely to me that such an odd morphological error would be made – unless it was by Gaelic speakers who were borrowing it because of its similarity to *sgonn*.

The eighteenth-century Gaelic poem using *sgonn* of a knife handle can be found in Black, *An Lasair*, 14. The 1848 text about a shinty game is in MacLeod, *Caraid nan Gaidheal*, 402. The song about the cheese in the shop window is given in MacFadyen, *An t-Eileanach*, 39. My translation.

The traditional proverb from Nova Scotia can be found in *Fear na Céilidh* 1.9 (November 1928): 72.

Bothy

The history of the Mountain Bothies Association can be found on their website at https://www.mountainbothies.org.uk/about-the-mba/mba-history/

An up-to-date discussion of the bothy ballads can be found in Olson, "Bothy Ballads," 326-28.

The history of the word "bothy" in Lowland Scots is discussed in Pödör, "Scottish Gaelic Loanwords," 178-79, *Oxford English Dictionary*, "bothy" and *Dictionary of the Scots Language*, "bothy."

The song-poem "*Bothan Àirigh am Bràighe Raineach*" can be found in McLeod and Newton, *An Ubhal as Àirde*, 389-91.

Pet

The history of the occurrences of the word "pet" in Lowland Scots and English can be found in *Oxford English Dictionary*, "pet," *Dictionary of the Scots Language*, "pet" and Breeze, "Notes On Some Scottish Words," 35-36. A discussion about how scholars have interpreted the origins of "pet" can be found in Liberman, "No Subject is Too Petty."

The Old Gaelic tale is "Aided tri Mac Nechta Sceni," quoted in *Electronic Dictionary of the Irish Language*, "petta." Discussion of animals in the Early

Irish laws can be found in Kelly, *Early Irish Farming*, 124-25. The quote from Keating can be found in *Electronic Dictionary of the Irish Language*, "petta."

The relationship between Gaelic *peata* and Welsh *peth* is discussed in O'Rahilly, *Early Irish History*, 356. The quote by Simon Taylor about the Book of Deer can be found in Taylor, "The toponymic landscape," 282-83.

The song by Alasdair mac Mhaighstir Alasdair can be found in Thomson, *Alasdair mac Mhaighstir Alasdair*, 38. The tale *Am Peata Bàn* can be found in Campbell, *Popular Tales of the West Highlands*, vol. 1, 194-99. This folktale type is classified as Aarne-Thompson code AT-130.

Caber

A discussion of the history and meaning of the word "caber" can be found in *Dictionary of the Scots Language*, "caber" and *Oxford English Dictionary*, "caber."

The description of tossing the caber in Strathglass in 1655 can be found in MacKay, *Chronicles of the Frasers*, 416. The practical skills related to cabers involved in building houses are discussed in Grant, *Highland Folk Ways*, 345.

The history of the song "Cabar Féidh" and the quatrain quoted can be found in Black, *An Lasair*, 110-11, 412-18. A discussion of the development of the bagpipe and fiddle tunes based on the melody is discussed in Gibson, *Old and New World Highland Bagpiping*, 175-76 and Lamb, *Keith Norman MacDonald's Puirt-à-Beul*, 159.

The expression about silk on a caber is in *Am Faclair Beag*.

Ingle

A discussion of the history of the word "ingle" can be found in *Oxford English Dictionary*, "ingle" and *Dictionary of the Scots Language*, "ingle."

The use of the word *aingeal* in the poetry of Iain Lom MacDonald can be found in MacKenzie, *Òrain Iain Luim*, 176. Lhuyd's references to the word *aingeal* can be found in Campbell and Thomson, *Edward Lhuyd*, 223, 224. The use of this word by Duncan Bàn can be found in MacLeod, *Òrain Dhonnchaidh Bhàin*, 18, 80, 224.

The quote from Alexander Carmichael can be found in Carmichael, *Carmina Gadelica*, vol. 2, 223.

Bog

A discussion of the types of bogs in Scotland can be found in Ferretto, et. al., "Potential carbon loss," 2101. The use of peat from bogs is discussed in Grant, *Highland Folk Ways*, 155, 159-60, 199-201.

Crag

The history of the word "crag" can be found in *Dictionary of the Scots Language*, "crag." The quote from Macky is given in McKim, "'Wild Men' and 'Wild Notions'," 129.

Information about the surname Craig can be found in Black, *The Surnames of Scotland*, 178-80.

Loch

Information about the name of the Lake of Menteith can be found in Newton, *Bho Chluaidh*, 74, 158 and Aitchison, "The Laich o' Menteith," 17.

The quote from William J. Watson can be found in Watson, *Scottish Place-Name Papers*, 51.

The episode about St. Columba and the Loch Ness monster can be found in Sharpe, *The Life of Columba*, 175-76. The quote from John Gregorson Campbell can be found in Black, *The Gaelic Otherworld*, 109.

Dulse

The opening discussion about the nutrients and virtues of dulse is from Chaey, "Seaweed, Aisle 4." The quote from Martin Martin can be found in Martin, *A Description of the Western Isles*, 149. Further discussion of the properties and uses of dulse can be found in Milliken and Bridgewater, *Flora Celtica*, 16, 52, 221, 228, 229, 231.

Discussion of the history of the word "dulse" can be found in *Oxford English Dictionary*, "dulse."

The quote about Highlanders chewing dulse can be found in Milliken and Bridgewater, *Flora Celtica*, 113. Carrageen is discussed at 51.

The twelfth-century Gaelic poem about St. Columba is from McLeod and Newton, *An Ubhal as Àirde*, 56, 58. The quatrain about what to eat in each season is given in Smith, *Aithris is Oideas*, 25. My translation.

Ptarmigan

For information about the ptarmigan from Gaelic tradition, see Forbes, *Gaelic Names*, 322 and Carmichael, *Ortha nan Gàidheal*, vol. 2, 368. The expressions about ptarmigans are taken from MacDhomhnaill, *An Ceathramh Leabhar Leughaidh*, 101.

For a discussion of the history of the word "ptarmigan" in Lowland Scots, see *Dictionary of the Scots Language*, "termigan" and "tarmagan."

The excerpt from the poem by Archibald Campbell (Gilleaspuig Caimbeul) is taken from Caimbeul, *Òrain le Gilleaspuig Caimbeul*, 22. My translation.

Galore

For discussion of the history of the word in English and Lowland Scots, see *Oxford English Dictionary*, "galore" and *Dictionary of the Scots Language*, "galore."

Grotty, Grody

A discussion of the history of the word "grotty" can be found in *Oxford English Dictionary*, "grotty."

The anecdote printed in 1876 can be found in *An Gàidheal* 5.55 (1876): 175. The Gaelic letter written in 1901 can be found in *Mac-Talla* 10.2 (12 July 1901): 14. My translation.

Gob

For discussion of the history of the word "gob" in English and Lowland Scots, see *Oxford English Dictionary*, "gob" and *Dictionary of the Scots Language*, "gob." See also *Am Faclair Beag*, "gob."

Cosy, Cozy

For a history of the word "cosy" in Lowland Scots and English, see *Dictionary of the Scots Language*, "cosy" and *Wiktionary*, "cosy." The proposal of its derivation from Gaelic *còs* is mentioned in Mackay, "Gaelic Words," 330.

The definitions of *còs*, *còsach*, *còsag*, *còsagach* and *còsan* are from entries in the dictionary compiled by Edward Dwelly in the early twentieth century, correlating directly to entries in earlier dictionaries, such as the two-volume set published in 1839 by MacLeod and Dewar. It is worth adding that fieldworker George Moss collected the variant form *cùsanach* "tranquil, quiet; stationary" in Strathglass, as detailed in the DASG archive.

The description of First Nations hunting practices is from McDougall, *Ceann-Iùil an Fhir-Imrich*, 38. My translation.

Snazzy

The history of the word "snazzy" in English is discussed in *Oxford English Dictionary*, "snazzy."

The fourteenth-century Gaelic poem can be found in McLeod and Newton, *An Ubhal as Àirde*, 84, 88. The Gaelic text of the poem by Alasdair mac Mhaighstir Alasdair can be found in Thomson, *Alasdair mac Mhaighstir Alasdair*, 44. My translation.

Information about George Harry Snazel can be found on the website for *Opera Scotland* http://www.operascotland.org/person/3375/George-Snazelle Two newspaper articles about Snazel referring to him as "Snazzy" are *Evening Post*, vol. LXI, issue 75, 30 March 1901 and *Otago Witness*, Dunedin, 15 April

1903. Arguments against "snazzy" being based on his name can be found on the Wiktionary in the Talk page about the word "snazzy."

For information about Gaelic speakers in San Francisco, see Newton, "'Becoming Cold-hearted'," 65, 85, 89-90, 92, 95, 110, 116, 124. The quote from the Gael in the city is from *The Celtic Monthly* 15 (1907): 38. My translation.

Brash

For a discussion of the word "brash" in English, see *Oxford English Dictionary*, "brash." The entry in the 1824 book can be found in Carr, *Horæ Momenta Cravenæ*, 61. A discussion of the relationship between "brash" and similar-sounding words in Germanic languages can be found in Liberman, "Face to Face with Brash: part 2."

Usages of the word *bras* in Gaelic can be gleaned from *Electronic Dictionary of the Irish Language*, "bras." The occurrence in *Tecosca Cormaic* can be found in the edition published in the online archive *CELT: Corpus of Electronic Texts* at https://celt.ucc.ie/published/T503001.html

For the appearance of *bras* in the poem by Maol-Domhnaigh Morrison, see McLeod and Bateman, *Duanaire na Sracaire*, 36. For the occurrence in the elegy for Sir Lachlann MacLean, see McLeod and Newton, *An Ubhal as Àirde*, 230, 234. For the elegy by Niall MacMhuirich, see Black, "The Poetry of Niall MacMhuirich," 287.

The occurrence in the song from the 1715 Rising can be found in Black, *An Lasair*, 38. The occurrence in the erotic poem by Alasdair mac Mhaighstir Alasdair can be found in Thomson, *Alasdair mac Mhaighstir Alasdair*, 63 and Black, *An Lasair*, 128-29. The prose dialog can be found in Kidd, *Comhraidhean nan Cnoc*, 133.

Dour

A history of the word "dour" in Lowland Scots can be found in *Dictionary of the Scots Language*, "dour." Its expansion in English is covered by *Oxford English Dictionary*, "dour." The usages and meanings of *dùr* in the medieval period can be gleaned from *Electronic Dictionary of the Irish Language*, "dúr."

The argument that "dour" is a borrowing from Gaelic into English, and the problems with a direct borrowing from Latin or French, is discussed in Sayers, "Dour: Etymology."

The use of *dùr* to describe Saxons in a Gaelic poem can be found, and is discussed, in Wadden, "The beauty and lust of the Gaels," 87, 89-90, 92-93.

The usage in the sixteenth-century poem in praise of Eòin MacGregor can be found in Watson, *Bardachd Albannach*, 214-15. The word appears in the poem by Am Bard Mac an t-Saoir in McLeod and Newton, *An Ubhal as Àirde*, 140, 142. The example in the poem by Uilleam Ros can be found in MacKenzie,

Sàr Obair, 296. My translation. The example from Nova Scotia can be found in MacGregor, *Dàin a Chomhnadh Cràbhuidh*, 32. My translation.

Jilt

Information about the history of the word "jilt" can be found in *Oxford English Dictionary*, "jilt" and Wiktionary, "jilt."

The history and usages of the Gaelic word *diùlt* can be gleaned from *Electronic Dictionary of the Irish Language*, "dilt." The example of describing guns as not misfiring using *diùlt* can be found in MacKenzie, *Òrain Iain Luim*, 2 (dated to 1618). The long excerpt from the love song can be found in Campbell and Collinson, *Hebridean Folksongs*, vol. 3, 128-31.

Information about Scottish immigrants in London after the 1603 Union of Crowns can be found in Brown and Kennedy, "Land of Opportunity?," 715, 725.

Glom

A discussion of the history and origins of the word "glom" in English and Lowland Scots can be found in *Oxford English Dictionary*, "glom" and *Dictionary of the Scots Language*, "glaum."

The quote from the Gaelic journal in 1917 can be found in MacBheathain, "Buaidh na Gàidhlig," 19.

Smidge, Smidgen

A discussion of the history and derivation of the word "smidge" in English and Lowland Scots can be found in *Dictionary of the Scots Language*, "smitch" and "smite" and *Oxford English Dictionary*, "smitch."

The poem "Soraidh slán don oidhche a-rér" and detailed analysis of it can be found in Clancy, "Reading Niall Mór MacMhuirich," 111-19.

The reconstructed form *smidean* is very rare in Scottish Gaelic because *smid* by itself already implies smallness. The meaning of *smidean*, however, is immediately obvious to Gaelic speakers and it may be that the Gaelic words that survived in the Lowland Scots vernacular of an area such as Ayrshire, where Gaelic died as a community language in the later eighteenth century, were used in a looser sense than they would have been in an area where the nuances of Gaelic remained better understood.

For discussion about the usage and derivation of "smithereens" in English, see Wiktionary, "smithereens."

Spunk

For a discussion of the history of the word "spunk" in English and Lowland Scots, see *Dictionary of the Scots Language*, "spunk" and "sponk" and

Liberman, "Real 'Spunk'." For discussion of the derivation of the term from Gaelic, see Sayers, "Challenges for English Etymology," 6-7.

The expression *cho tioram ri spuing* can be found in Forbes, *Gaelic Names of Plants*, 41. The excerpt describing tasks done during a *céilidh* can be found in Ross, "Old Highland Industries," 394. The collection of fungus as fire-starters can be found in Forbes, *Gaelic Names of Plans*, 99.

Bore

A discussion of the history of the word "bore" in English is given in *Oxford English Dictionary*, "bore."

The excerpt from the poem by Sìleas na Ceapaich can be found in Black, *An Lasair*, 22. My translation. The excerpt from the 1840s text can be found in Whyte, *Leabhar na Céilidh*, 90-91. My translation.

The usages and meanings of the Gaelic terms can be gleaned from the entries in *Electronic Dictionary of the Irish Language*, "bodraid." There is discussion about the borrowings of *bodhar* and the forms that they have taken in English in *Dictionary of the Scots Language*, "bather" and Liberman, "Why Bother?"

The quote by Patrick Joyce can be found in Joyce, *Irish Names*, 47.

Dig, Twig

Discussion of the early uses of the slang phrase "Can you dig it?" can be found on the blog post http://pancocojams.blogspot.com/2014/09/can-you-dig-it-in-records-movies-1969.html

Discussion of the origins of the word "dig" can be found on Wiktionary, "dig." A related discussion of the word "twig" can be found in *Oxford English Dictionary*, "twig." Discussion about its derivation in Gaelic can be found in MacBheathain, "Buaidh na Gàidhlig," 19-20, Hamp, "On the Celtic origin," Sayers, "Challenges for English Etymology," 5-6, Carey, "Can you twig it?," and MacIlleathain, *Leabhar nan Litrichean*, 239.

Bibliography

All URLs were accessed in the year 2020.

AITCHISON, NICK. "The Laich o' Menteith: reassessing the origins of the Lake of Menteith." *The Journal of Scottish Name Studies* 10 (2016): 1-24.

ALBURGER, MARY ANNE. *Scottish Fiddlers and their Music.* London: Victor Gollancz, 1983.

- "The Fiddle." In *Oral Literature and Performance Culture: Scottish Life and Society,* vol. 10, edited by John Beech, et. al., 238-73. Edinburgh: John Donald, 2007.

ALEXANDER, HENRY. *The Cairngorms.* Edinburgh: The Scottish Mountaineering Club, 1928.

ALLARDYCE, ALEXANDER, ed. *Scotland and Scotsmen in the Eighteenth Century,* 2 vols. Edinburgh and London: W. Blackwood and Sons, 1888.

ANON. *The Loch Lomond Expedition, with Some Short Reflections on the Perth Manifesto.* Glasgow, 1715.

BANNERMAN, JOHN. "The Scots Language and the Kin-based Society." In *Gaelic and Scots in Harmony,* edited by Derick Thomson, 1-19. Glasgow: University of Glasgow, 1988.

BARRETT, GRANT. "Humdinger of a Bad Scholar." https://grantbarrett.com/humdinger-of-a-bad-irish-scholar/

BARROW, G. W. S. "The lost Gàidhealtachd of medieval Scotland." In *Gaelic and Scotland / Alba agus a' Ghàidhlig,* edited by William Gillies, 67-88. Edinburgh: Edinburgh University Press, 1989.

BLACK, GEORGE. *The Surnames of Scotland: Their Origin, Meaning, and History.* New York: New York Public Library, 1946.

BLACK, RONALD. "The Poetry of Niall MacMhuirich." *Transactions of the Gaelic Society of Inverness* 46 (1971): 281-307.

- ed. *An Lasair: Anthology of 18th-Century Scottish Gaelic Verse.* Edinburgh: Birlinn, 2001.

- ed. *The Gaelic Otherworld.* Edinburgh: Birlinn, 2005.

- "Appendix 3: Smeòrach Chlann Raghnaill: The Mavis of Clanranald." In *Alexander MacDonald: Bard of the Gaelic Enlightenment,* edited by Camille Dressler and Domhnall Stiùbhart, 139-42. South Lochs, Isle of Lewis: The Islands Book Trust, 2012.

BREEZE, ANDREW. "Celtic etymologies for Old English *cursung* 'curse,' *gafeluc* 'javelin,' *staer* 'history,' *syrce* 'coat of mail,' and Middle English *clog(ge)* 'block, wooden shoe,' *cokkunge* 'striving,' *tirven* 'to flay,' *warroke* 'hunchback.' " *Notes and Queries* 40.3 (1993): 287-89.

- "Irish Beltaine 'May Day' and Beltancu, a Cattle Rent in pre-Norman Lancashire." *Éigse* 29 (1996): 59-63.
- "Scots Fary, 'Tumult' and Gaelic Faire, 'Look Out!'" *Scottish Gaelic Studies* 23 (2007): 53-56.
- "Notes on Scottish words and phrases: Mugdock, ploddeil, hallock, 'derb dan', 'carlingis pet'." *Scottish Language* 28 (2009): 27-38.
- "Gaelic Vocabulary." In *The Edinburgh Companion to the Gaelic Language*, edited by Moray Watson and Michelle Macleod, 218-28. Edinburgh: Edinburgh University Press, 2010.

BROWN, KEITH AND ALLAN KENNEDY. "Land of Opportunity? The Assimilation of Scottish Migrants in England, 1603-ca. 1762." *Journal of British Studies* 57.4 (October 2018): 709-35.

BUCHANAN, WILLIAM. *Account of the Family of Buchanan.* Glasgow, 1733.

CAIMBEUL, GILLEASBUIG. *Òrain le Gilleaspuig Caimbeul, Ceann Loch Earn.* Edinburgh: MacIain agus Hunter, 1851.

CALDWELL, DAVID. "Having the right kit: West Highlanders fighting in Ireland." In *The World of the Galloglass: Kings, warlords and warriors in Ireland and Scotland, 1200-1600*, edited by Séan Duffy, 144-68. Dublin: Four Courts Press, 2007.

CAMPBELL, JOHN F., ed. *Leabhar na Féinne, vol. 1: Gaelic Texts.* London: Spottiswoode, 1872.

CAMPBELL, JOHN G. *The Fians.* London: David Nutt, 1891.

CAMPBELL, JOHN L., ed. *A Collection of Highland Rites and Customes.* Cambridge: D. S. Brewer, 1975.

- ed. *Òrain Ghàidhealach mu Bhliadhna Theàrlaich / Highland Songs of the Forty-Five, Scottish Gaelic Texts 15.* Edinburgh: Scottish Gaelic Texts Society, 1984 [1933].
- *A Very Civil People: Hebridean Folk, History and Tradition*, ed. Hugh Cheape. Edinburgh: Birlinn, 2000.
- and Francis Collinson, eds. *Hebridean Folksongs*, 3 vols. Oxford: Oxford University Press, 1969-1981.
- and Derick S. Thomson, eds. *Edward Lhuyd in the Scottish Highlands, 1699-1700.* Oxford: Clarendon Press, 1963.

CAREY, JOHN. *The Irish National Origin-Legend: Synthetic Pseudohistory.* Cambridge: University of Cambridge, 1994.

CAREY, STAN. "Can you twig it?" MacMillan Dictionary Blog. http://www.macmillandictionaryblog.com/can-you-twig-it

CARMICHAEL, ALEXANDER, ed. *Ortha nan Gàidheal / Carmina Gadelica*, 6 vols. Edinburgh: Scottish Gaelic Texts Society, 1900-71.

CARNEY, JAMES. *Medieval Irish Lyrics with The Irish Bardic Poet.* Dublin: The Dolmen Press, 1985.

CARR, WILLIAM. *Horæ Momenta Cravenæ: Or, The Craven Dialect, Exemplified in Two Dialogues*. London: Hurst, Robinson and Co., 1824.

CHAEY, CHRISTINA. "Seaweed, Aisle 4: Why This Bacon-Flavored Superfood Could Be the Next Kale." *bon appéitit* 30 July 2015 https://www.bonappetit.com/test-kitchen/ingredients/article/dulse-seaweed

CHEAPE, HUGH. "Gheibhte Breacain Chàrnaid ('Scarlet Tartans Would Be Got ...'): The Re-invention of Tradition." In *From Tartan To Tartanry*, edited by Ian Brown, 13-31. Edinburgh: Edinburgh University Press, 2010.

CLANCY, THOMAS OWEN. "A Fond Farewell to Last Night's Literary Criticism: Reading Niall Mór MacMhuirich." In *Cànan & Cultar / Language & Culture: Rannsachadh na Gàidhlig 4*, edited by Gillian Munro and Richard Cox, 109-125. Edinburgh: Dunedin Academic Press, 2010.

DEWAR, JOHN. *The Dewar Manuscripts, Volume One*, ed. John MacKechnie. Glasgow: William MacLellan, 1964.

DOSSENA, MARINA. "'Sassenach', eh? Late Modern Scottish English on the borders of time and space." *Token: A Journal of English Linguistics* 7 (2018): 53-76.

DUFFY, SEÁN. "The prehistory of the galloglass." In *The World of the Galloglass: Kings, wardlords and warriors in Ireland and Scotland, 1200-1600*, edited by Seán Duffy, 1-23. Dublin: Four Courts Press, 2007.

DURKIN, PHILIP. *Borrowed words: a history of loanwords in English*. Oxford: Oxford University Press, 2014.

EPSTEIN, DENA J. *Sinful Tunes and Spirituals: Black Folk Music to the Civil War*. Urbana: University of Illinois Press, 1977.

EVANS, DEWI AND BRYNLEY ROBERTS, eds. *Edward Lhwyd: Archæologia Britannica*. Aberystwyth: Celtic Studies Publications, 2009.

FERRETTO, ANNA, ROB BROOKER, MATT AITKENHEAD, ROBIN MATTHEWS AND PETE SMITH. "Potential carbon loss from Scottish peatlands under climate change." *Regional Environmental Change* 19 (2019): 2101-11.

FLETT, J. F. AND T. M. FLETT. *Traditional Step-Dancing in Scotland*. Edinburgh: Scottish Cultural Press, 1996.

FORBES, ALEXANDER. *Gaelic Names of Beasts (Mammalia), Birds, Fishes, Insects, Reptiles, etc.* Edinburgh: Oliver and Boyd, 1905:

FORBES, ROBERT. *The Lyon in mourning; or, A collection of speeches, letters, journals, etc. relative to the affairs of Prince Charles Edward Stuart*, 3 vols. Edinburgh: Scottish History Society, 1895-96.

FOSTER, SALLY. *Picts, Gaels and Scots*. London: Historic Scotland, 2004.

FRASER, SIMON. *The Airs and Melodies Peculiar to the Highlands of Scotland and the Isles*. Inverness: H. Mackenzie, 1874 [1815].

FRENCH, MORVERN. "The Flemish Influence on Scottish Language." 2014. https://flemish.wp.st-andrews.ac.uk/2014/05/09/the-flemish-influence-on-scottish-language/

GHRIOGAIR, SEÒNAID. *Ri Luinneig mun Chrò: Crodh ann am Beatha agus Dualchas nan Gàidheal.* Crieff: Grace Note Publications, 2014.

GIBSON, JOHN. *Old and New World Highland Bagpiping.* Edinburgh: Birlinn, 2005.

GOLDIE, DAVID AND RODERICK WATSON, eds. *From the Line: Scottish War Poetry 1914-1945.* Glasgow: Association for Scottish Literary Studies, 2014.

GRAHAM, PATRICK. *Sketches of Perthshire.* 2nd ed. Edinburgh: James Ballantyne, 1912.

GRANT, I. F. *Highland Folk Ways.* London: Routledge, 1961.

- and Hugh Cheape. *Periods in Highland History.* New York, Barnes and Noble: 2000.

GRIMMER, MARTIN. "Columban Christian Influence in Northumbria, before and after Whitby." *Journal of the Australian Early Medieval Association* 4 (2008): 99-123.

HAMMOND, MATTHEW. "Introduction: The Study of Personal Names in Medieval Scotland." In *Personal Names and Naming Practices in Medieval Scotland,* edited by Matthew Hammond, 1-17. Woodbridge: Boydell Press, 2019.

HAMP, ERIC. "On the Celtic origin of English slang dig/twig 'understand'." *Comments on Etymology* 10.12 (1981): 2-3.

HISKEY, DAVEN. "Why Are The Academy Awards Statues Called Oscars?" Mental Floss 2013/2019 https://www.mentalfloss.com/article/48892/why-are-academy-awards-statuettes-called-oscars

HOUSEWRIGHT, WILEY L. *A History of Music and Dance in Florida, 1565-1865.* Tuscaloosa: University of Alabama Press, 1991.

HUNTER, MICHAEL. *The Occult Laboratory: Magic, Science and Second Sight in Late Seventeenth-Century Scotland.* Woodbridge: Boydell Press, 2001.

HUTSON, ARTHUR. "Gaelic Loan-Words in American." *American Speech* 22.2 (1947): 18-23.

JOYCE, PATRICK. *Irish Names of Places,* 2 vols. Dublin: Phoenix Publishing Co., 1875.

KELLY, FERGUS. *Early Irish Farming.* Dublin: Dublin Institute for Advanced Studies, 1997.

KIDD, COLIN. "Teutonic Ethnology and Scottish Nationalist Inhibition, 1780-1880." *The Scottish Historical Review* 74 (1995): 45-68.

KIDD, SHEILA, ed. *Còmhraidhean nan Cnoc: the Nineteenth-Century Gaelic Prose Dialogue.* Edinburgh: Scottish Gaelic Texts Society, 2016.

- "Kangaroos and Cockatoos: Gaelic Literature in the Nineteenth-Century Antipodes." *Scottish Literary Review* 9.2 (2017): 1-18.

KNOTT, ELEANOR. "Filidh Éireann Go Haointeach." *Ériu* 5 (1911): 50-69.

KOCH, JOHN. "Ériu, Alba, and Letha: When was a Language Ancestral to Gaelic First Spoken in Ireland?" *Emania* 9 (1991): 17-27.

- ed. *Celtic Culture: A Historical Encyclopedia*, 5 vols. Santa Barbara: ABC-CLIO, 2005.

LAMB, WILLIAM. "Reeling in the Strathspey: The Origins of Scotland's National Music." *Scottish Studies* 36 (2011-13): 66-102.

- ed. *Keith Norman MacDonald's Puirt-à-Beul: The Vocal Dance Music of the Scottish Gaels*. Upper Breakish, Skye: Taigh na Teud, 2012.

- "Grafting Culture: On the Development and Diffusion of the Strathspey in Scottish Music." *Scottish Studies* 37 (2014): 94-104.

LIBERMAN, ANATOLY. "Blessing and cursing, part 3: curse (conclusion)." https://blog.oup.com/2016/11/curse-etymology/

- "Face to face with brash: part 2." https://blog.oup.com/2017/02/etymology-brash-continued/

- "Multifarious devils, part 1: 'bogey'." https://blog.oup.com/2013/05/bogey-word-origin-etymology/

- "No Subject is Too Petty for an Etymologist, Or, Pets from North to South." https://blog.oup.com/2009/04/pets/

- "Real 'spunk'." https://blog.oup.com/2012/07/word-origin-spunk-punk-funk/

- "Why bother?." https://blog.oup.com/2017/03/bother-word-origin/

LUCAS, A. T. *Cattle in Ancient Ireland*. Kilkenny: Boethius Press, 1989.

MACBHEATHAIN, LACHLANN. "Buaidh na Gàidhlig air Beurla nan Gall." *An Ròsarnach* 1.2 (1917): 16-33.

MACCHOINNICH, IAIN. *Eachdraidh a' Phrionnsa, no Bliadhna Thearlaich*. Paisley: Alasdair Gardner, 1906 [1845].

MACDHOMHNAILL, IAIN, ed. *An Ceathramh Leabhar Leughaidh*. Glasgow: Blackie and Son, 1923.

MACDHONNCHAIDH, AONGHAS. *An t-Ogha Mór, no Am fear-sgeòil air uilinn*. Glasgow: MacDhonnchaidh, Ueir & Co., 1913.

MACDONALD, ALEXANDER. "Shinty: Historical and Traditional." *Transactions of the Gaelic Society of Inverness* 30 (1924): 27-56.

MACDOUGALL, JAMES AND GEORGE CALDER. *Folk Tales and Fairy Lore*. Edinburgh: John Grant, 1910.

MACFADYEN, JOHN. *An t-Eileanach*. Glasgow: Archibald Sinclair, 1890.

MACGREGOR, JAMES. *Dàin a Chomhnadh Cràbhuidh*. Glasgow: Young and Galie, 1819.

MACGREGOR, MARTIN. "Gaelic Barbarity and Scottish Identity in the Later Middle Ages." In *Mìorun Mòr nan Gall, 'The Great Ill-Will of the Lowlander'? Lowland Perceptions of the Highlands, Medieval and Modern*, edited by Dauvit Broun and Martin MacGregor, 7-48. Glasgow: University of Glasgow, 2007.

MacILLEATHAIN, RUAIRIDH. *Leabhar nan Litrichean.* Inverness: Clì Gàidhlig, 2005.

MacINNES, ALLAN. *Clanship, Commerce and the House of Stuart, 1603-1788.* East Linton: Tuckwell Press, 1996.

MacINNES, JOHN. *Dùthchas nan Gàidheal: Selected Essays of John MacInnes,* ed. Michael Newton. Edinburgh: Birlinn, 2006.

MACKAY, CHARLES. *The Gaelic Etymology of the Languages of Western Europe.* London: Trübner, 1877.

MACKAY, WILLIAM. "Celtic Words Borrowed By The English." *The Celtic Magazine* 13 (1888): 327-33.

- ed. *Chronicles of the Frasers. The Wardlaw Manuscript.* Edinburgh: Scottish History Society, 1905.

MacKENZIE, ANNIE, ed. *Òrain Iain Luim / Songs of John MacDonald, Bard of Keppoch, Scottish Gaelic Texts 8.* Edinburgh: Scottish Gaelic Texts Society, 1964.

MacKENZIE, JAMES. *The History of Scotland.* London: T. Nelson and Sons, 1867.

MacKENZIE, JOHN, ed. *Sàr-Obair nam Bard Gäelach; or, the Beauties of Gaelic Poetry.* Glasgow: MacGregor, Polson, & Co, 1841.

MacKILLOP, JAMES. *Oxford Dictionary of Celtic Mythology.* Oxford: Oxford University Press, 1998.

MacLENNAN, HUGH DAN. "Shinty's Place and Space in the World." *The Sports Historian* 18.1 (May 1998): 1-23.http://www.uscamanachd.org/documents/MacLennan_Shintysplace.pdf

MacLEOD, ANGUS ed. *Òrain Dhonnchaidh Bhàin / The Songs of Duncan Ban Macintyre.* Edinburgh: Scottish Gaelic Texts Society, 1978.

MacLEOD, DONALD. *Memoirs of the Life and Gallant Exploits of the Old Highlander, Serjeant Donald Macleod.* London: Peterborough-House Press, 1791.

MacLEOD, NORMAN. *Caraid nan Gaidheal: The Friend of the Gael,* ed. A. Clark. Edinburgh: John Grant, 1910.

MacLEÒID, DOMHNUL. *Òrain Nuadh Ghaeleach.* Inverness: John Young, 1811.

MacMILLAN, SOMHAIRLE, ed. *Sporan Dhomhnaill: Gaelic Poems and Songs of the late Donald Macintyre.* Edinburgh: Scottish Gaelic Texts Society, 1968.

MacPHAIL, J. R. N., ed. *Highland Papers,* 3 vols. Edinburgh: Scottish History Society, 1914-1920.

MARTIN, MARTIN. *A Description of the Western Islands of Scotland.* London, 1716.

MATHESON, WILLIAM. ed. *An Clàrsair Dall / The Blind Harper.* Edinburgh: Scottish Gaelic Texts Society, 1970.

- *Highland Surnames.* Inverness: An Comunn Gàidhealach, 1973.

McCONE, KIM. *The Celtic Question: Modern Constructs and Ancient Realities.* Dublin: Dublin Institute for Advanced Studies, 2008.

McDOUGALL, ROBERT. *Ceann-Iùil an Fhir-Imrich.* Glasgow: J & P Campbell, 1841.

McKim, Anne. "'Wild Men' and 'Wild Notions': Challenging Prejudices about Scotland in Early Eighteenth-Century Travel Writing." In *What Countrey's This? And Whither Are We Gone?": Papers presented at the Twelfth International Conference on the Literature of Region and Nation*, edited by J. Derrick McClure, Karoline Szatek-Tudor, Rosa E. Penna, 118-34. Cambridge: Cambridge Scholars Publishing, 2010.

McLeod, Wilson. "Gaelic Poetry as Historical Source: Some Problems and Possibilities." In *Ireland (Ulster) Scotland: Concepts, Contexts, Comparisons*, edited by Edna Longley, Eamonn Hughes and Des O'Rawe, 171-79. Belfast: Queen's University, 2003.

- *Divided Gaels: Gaelic Cultural Identities in Scotland and Ireland, c.1200-c.1650*. Oxford: Oxford University Press, 2004.

- and Meg Bateman, eds. *Duanaire na Sracaire / Songbook of the Pillagers: Anthology of Medieval Gaelic Poetry*. Edinburgh: Birlinn, 2007.

- and Michael Newton, eds. *An Ubhal as Àirde / The Highest Apple: An Anthology of Scottish Gaelic Literature*. Francis Boutle: London, 2019.

Meek, Donald. "Gàidhlig is Gaylick anns na Meadhan Aoisean." In *Gaelic and Scotland / Alba agus a' Ghàidhlig*, edited by William Gillies, 131-45. Edinburgh: Edinburgh University Press, 1989.

- ed. *Màiri Mhòr nan Òran: Taghadh de a h-Òrain*. Edinburgh: Comann Litreachas Gàidhlig na h-Alba, 1998.

- "The Gaelic Literary Enlightenment: The Making of the Scottish Gaelic New Testament and Associated Books, 1750-1820 - The O'Donnell Lecture, 2018." http://meekwrite.blogspot.com/2018/06/the-gaelic-literary-enlightenment.html

Melin, Mats. *A Story to Every Dance: The role of lore in enhancing the Scottish solo dance tradition*. Lorg Press, 2018.

Milliken, William and Sam Bridgewater. *Flora Celtica: Plants and People in Scotland*. Edinburgh: Birlinn, 2004.

Morgan, Ailig Peadar. *Ethnonyms in the Place-names of Scotland and the Border Counties of England*. Unpublished Ph.D. dissertation, University of Edinburgh, 2011.

Muhr, Kim. "Bealtine in Irish and Scottish Place-names." *The Journal of Scottish Name Studies* 10 (2016): 89-126.

Newton, Michael. " 'Becoming Cold-hearted like the Gentiles Around Them': Scottish Gaelic in the United States 1872-1912," *e-Keltoi: Journal of Interdisciplinary Celtic Studies* 2 (2003): 63-131.

- "The Fiery Cross: Folklore, Literature and Fakelore." *History Scotland* (May/June 2005): 34-39.

- *Bho Chluaidh gu Calasraid / From the Clyde to Callander: Gaelic Songs, Poetry, Tales and Traditions of the Lennox and Menteith in Gaelic with English translations*. Glasgow: Zetivula, 2010 [1999].
- " 'Did you hear about the Gaelic-speaking African?': Scottish Gaelic Folklore about Identity in North America." *Comparative American Studies* 8.2 (2010): 88-106.
- "'Dannsair air ùrlar-déile thu': Gaelic evidence about dance from the mid-17th to late-18th century Highlands." *International Review of Scottish Studies* 38 (2013): 49-78.
- *The Naughty Little Book of Gaelic: All of the Scottish Gaelic You Need to Curse, Swear, Drink, Smoke and Fool Around*. Sydney, Cape Breton: Cape Breton University Press, 2014.
- *The Everyday Life of the Clans of the Scottish Highlands*. Chapel Hill: Saorsa Media, 2020.
- AND HUGH CHEAPE. " 'The Keening of Women and the Roar of the Pipe' : From Clàrsach to Bagpipe (c. 1600 - 1782)." *Ars Lyrica* 17 (2008): 75-95.

NEWTE, THOMAS. *Prospects and Observations; On a Tour in England and Scotland: Natural Economical, and Literary*. London: G. G. J. and J Robinson., 1791.

NICOLSON, ALEXANDER. *Gaelic Proverbs*. Edinburgh: Birlinn, 1996 [1881].

Ó BAOILL, COLM ed. *Eachann Bacach agus Bàird Eile de Chloinn Ghill-Eathain / Eachann Bacach and Other MacLean Poets, Scottish Gaelic Texts 14*. Edinburgh: Scottish Gaelic Texts Society, 1979.

- ed. *Màiri nighean Alasdair Ruaidh: Song-maker of Skye and Berneray*. Edinburgh: Scottish Gaelic Texts Society, 2014.
- and Meg Bateman, eds. *Gàir nan Clàrsach / The Harp's Cry: An Anthology of 17th-century Gaelic Poetry*. Edinburgh: Birlinn Ltd, 1994.

Ó CATHASAIGH, TÓMAS. "The literature of medieval Ireland to c.800: St. Patrick to the Vikings." In *The Cambridge History of Irish Literature*, vol 1., edited by Margaret Kelleher and Philip O'Leary, 9-31. Cambridge: Cambridge University Press, 2006.

Ó CRÓINÍN, DÁIBHÍ. *Early Medieval Ireland, 400-1200*. London: Longman, 1995.

Ó CRUALAOICH, GEARÓID. *The Book of the Cailleach*. Cork: Cork University Press, 2003.

OLSON, IAN. "Bothy Ballads and Song." In *Oral Literature and Performance Culture*, edited by John Beech, et al, 322-59. Edinburgh: Birlinn, 2007.

Ó MAOLALAIGH, ROIBEARD. "DASG: Digital Archive of Scottish Gaelic / Dachaigh airson Stòras na Gàidhlig." *Scottish Gaelic Studies* 30 (2016): 242-62.

Ó RIAIN, PÁDRAIG. "Scottorum Origines Fabulosae: The Metz Version of Lebor Gabála Érenn." In *Lebor Gabála Érenn: Textual History and Pseudohistory*, edited by John Carey, 33-47. London: The Irish Texts Society, 2009.

O'Rahilly, Thomas. "Etymological Notes III." *Scottish Gaelic Studies* 3 (1931): 52-72.

- *Early Irish History and Mythology*. Dublin: Dublin Institute for Advanced Studies, 1946.

Pennant, Thomas. *A Tour in Scotland*. 1769. Chester: John Monk, 1771.

Pödör, Dóra. "The Phonology of Scottish Gaelic Loanwords in Lowland Scots." *Scottish Language* 14/15 (1995/96): 174-89.

Pons-Sanz, Sara and Aonghas MacCoinnich. "The Languages of Scotland." In *The International Companion to Scottish Literature 1400-1650*, edited by Nicola Ryan, 19-37. Glasgow: Scottish Literature International, 2018.

Ross, Alexander. "Old Highland Industries." *Transactions of the Gaelic Society of Inverness* 12 (1886): 387-415.

Safire, William. "On Language; My Name Ain't Mac, Buddy." *New York Times* 17 June 1984, section 6, page 6.

Sayers, William. "Challenges for English Etymology in the Twenty-First Century, with Illustrations." *Studia Neophilologica* 84:1 (2012): 1-25.

- "Scones, the OED, and the Celtic Element of English Vocabulary." *Notes & Queries* 52 (2005): 447-450.

- "Dour: Etymology." *Notes & Queries* 59 (2012): 337-38.

- "Challenges for English Etymology in the Twenty-First Century, with Illustrations." *Studia Neophilologica* 84:1 (2012): 1-25.

- "Two Scottish Etymologies for English Words." *Scottish Language* 35 (2016): 43-50.

Scott, Maggie. "Scots Word of the Season: 'Sassenach'." *The Imp* 13 (2013). https://www.thebottleimp.org.uk/2013/05/scots-word-of-the-season-sassenach/

Sellar, David. "The Family." In *A History of Everyday Life in Medieval Scotland, 1000 to 1600*, edited by Edward Cowan and Lizanne Henderson, 89-108. Edinburgh: Edinburgh University Press, 2011.

Sharpe, Richard, ed. *Life of St Columba*. London: Penguin Books, 1995.

Simms, Katherine. "Guesting and Feasting in Gaelic Ireland." *Journal of the Royal Society of Antiquaries of Ireland* 108 (1978): 67-100.

- "Images of Warfare in Bardic Poetry." *Celtica* 21 (1980): 608-19.

- *From Kings to Warlords*. Woodbridge: The Boydell Press, 1987.

- "Gaelic warfare in the Middle Ages." In *A Military History of Ireland*, edited by Thomas Bartlett and Keith Jeffery, 99-115. Cambridge: Cambridge University Press, 1996.

Simmons, Andrew, ed. *Burt's Letters from the North of Scotland*. Edinburgh: Birlinn, 1998 [1754].

Smibert, Thomas. *The Clans of the Highlands of Scotland*. Edinburgh: James Hogg, 1850.

SMITH, JEREMY. "Scots Language in Diana Gabaldon's 'Outlander'." *The Bottle Imp* 18 (2015). https://www.thebottleimp.org.uk/2015/06/scots-language-in-diana-gabaldons-outlander/

SMITH, JOHN, ed. *Aithris is Oideas: Traditional Gaelic Rhymes and Games.* London: University of London Press, 1964.

STIFTER, THOMAS. "Old Irish Etymology through the Ages." *Language and History* 1.63 (2020): 24-46.

TAYLOR, SIMON. "The toponymic landscape of the Gaelic Notes in the Book of Deer." In *Studies on the Book of Deer*, edited by Katherine Forsyth, 275-308. Dublin: Four Courts Press, 2008.

THIER, KATRIN. "Of Picts and Penguins - Celtic Languages in the New Edition of the Oxford English Dictionary." In *The Celtic Languages in Contact*, edited by Hildegard Tristram, 246-59. Potsdam University Press, 2007.

THOMSON, DERICK, ed. *The Companion to Gaelic Scotland.* Glasgow: Gairm, 1994.

- ed. *Alasdair mac Mhaighstir Alasdair: Selected Poems.* Edinburgh: The Scottish Gaelic Texts Society, 1996.

THOMSON, R. L. ed. *Foirm na h-Urrnuidheadh.* Edinburgh: Scottish Gaelic Texts Society, 1970.

WADDEN, PATRICK. " 'The beauty and lust of the Gaels'. National characteristics and medieval Gaelic learned culture." *North American Journal of Celtic Studies* 2.2 (2018): 85-104.

WATSON, WILLIAM J. "Personal Names: The Influence of the Saints." *Transactions of the Gaelic Society of Inverness* 32 (1929): 220-47.

- ed. *Bàrdachd Ghàidhlig: Specimens of Gaelic Poetry, 1550-1900*, 3rd ed. Stirling: An Comunn Gàidhealach, 1959.

- *Scottish Place-Name Papers.* London: Steve Savage, 2002.

WHYTE, HENRY. *Leabhar na Céilidh.* Glasgow: Archibald Sinclair, 1898.

WOOLF, ALEX. "The 'When, Why & Wherefore' of Scotland." *History Scotland* 2 (March 2002): 12-16.

- *From Pictland to Alba, 789-1070.* Edinburgh: Edinburgh University Press, 2007.

- "Reporting Scotland in the Anglo-Saxon Chronicle." In *Reading the Anglo-Saxon Chronicle*, edited by Alice Jorgensen, 221-39. Turnhout: Brepols, 2010.

About the Author

Dr Michael Newton earned a Ph.D. in Celtic Studies from the University of Edinburgh in 1998 and was an Assistant Professor in the Celtic Studies department of St Francis Xavier University in Nova Scotia 2008-2013. He has written a multitude of books and articles about Gaelic culture and history and is a leading authority on Scottish Gaelic heritage in North America.

In 2014 he was given the inaugural Saltire Award by the St. Andrews University Scottish Heritage Center (of Laurinburg, North Carolina) for his "outstanding contributions to the preservation and interpretation of Scottish history and culture." In 2018 he was recognized with the International award at the annual Scottish Gaelic awards in Glasgow, Scotland. In 2020, *An Ubhal as Àirde / The Highest Apple*, the first comprehensive anthology of Scottish Gaelic literature, which he edited with Wilson McLeod, was recognized as the Best Gaelic Non-fiction Book of the Year by the Gaelic Books Council in Scotland.

About the Illustrator

Natalia Lopes is an illustrator and comic artist living in Raleigh, North Carolina. Her specialties include black and white illustration and visual storytelling. Her work has been crowdfunded on Kickstarter as of 2019 and has been featured in blogs and independently published zines. You can find more of her work at mystopress.com.